DOG
FACTS

DOG FACTS

Joan Palmer

STANLEY
PAUL

A QUARTO BOOK

Stanley Paul & Co Ltd

An imprint of Random Century Ltd
20 Vauxhall Bridge Road
London SW1V 2SA

© Copyright 1991 Quarto Publishing plc

British Library Cataloguing-in-Publication Data
Palmer, Joan
Dog facts.
I. Title
636.7

ISBN 0-09-174879-8

This book was designed and produced by
Quarto Publishing plc
The Old Brewery
6 Blundell Street
London N7 9BH

Senior Editor Kate Kirby
Editor Helen Douglas-Cooper
Art Editor Anne Fisher
Designer Hazel Eddington
Illustrators Ray Hutchins, John Francis, Wayne Ford,
Sally Launder, Dave Kemp, Elly King

Picture Manager Sarah Risley
Art Director Nick Buzzard
Publishing Director Janet Slingsby

Typeset by ABC Typesetting Limited, Bournemouth
Manufactured in Singapore by Eray Scan Pte. Ltd
Printed in Singapore by Tien Wah Press (Pte.) Ltd.

CONTENTS

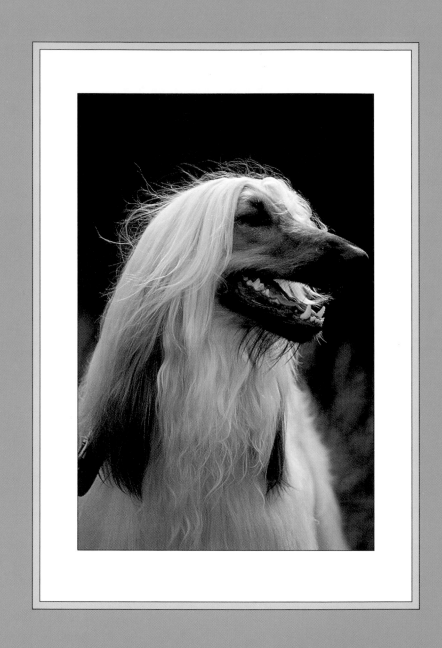

THE
NATURE
OF THE
DOG

WHEN DID DOGS ORIGINATE?

THE DOG, in common with wolves, foxes and jackals belongs to the family *Canidae*. This is one of seven families in the Carnivore, or meat-eating, order of mammals.

The evolution of the dog, *Canis familiaris*, traces back to a small, tree-climbing, weasel-like carnivore, the *Miacis*, which dwelt in forests 50 million years ago. A descendant of the *Miacis* was the *Tomarctus*, a small, fox-like creature, which appeared some 35 million years later and is generally acknowledged as the forerunner of the dog, wolf, fox and jackal. But the *Tomarctus* had disappeared by the middle of the Pleistocene age, about one million years ago, and by then, wolves and jackals were well established.

"WOLF IN SHEEP'S CLOTHING"

The saying that, "a dog is a wolf in sheep's clothing" is not far amiss. The most likely ancestor of the domestic dog is the grey wolf, with which it shares various characteristics. The jackal is another possibility. However it is unlikely that the dog could have evolved from the fox.

It is of interest that matings between a wolf and dog prove fertile – as do some between dog and jackal – and that the dog which escapes into the wild will revert to the wolf-like behaviour of its ancestors. Much of the behaviour patterns of the domestic dog today, particularly when in the company of its own kind, can be traced back to that of the wolf pack.

The dog family is often divided into two distinct groups, the dogs and wolves, and the foxes and jackals. Both have much in common. They are meat-eaters with 42 teeth. They have four or five toes on

Below *The genus* Canis *includes the wolf, jackal and fox, all of which were present in Europe, Asia and Africa in the Pliocene age 10 million years ago. They appeared in North America only 1 million years ago.*

Their forerunner, the Tomarctus, *would appear from its skull to have been*

similar to the modern dog. It was capable of speed, resembled the badger, and had a red coat and thick tail.

The wolf (Canis lupus), which appeared 500,000 years ago and was much smaller than the wolf of today, could well be the ancestor of the dog.

Miacis

Tomarctus

Left *The Egyptian god, Anubis, ruler of the dead, symbolized both the dog and the jackal. This mythological son of Osiris, God of the underworld, shows a remarkable resemblance to the Pharaoh Hound. It may be seen in the Louvre Museum, Paris. The Pharaoh Hound breed has changed little in 5,000 years.*

Right *The jackal* (Canis aureus), *a gregarious species, is renowned for its piercing wail. It is smaller than the wolf, bigger than the fox, and originates in tropical Asia. Crossbreedings of dogs with jackals have been claimed.*

their fore-feet, four on their hind-feet. They run on their toes, and their claws, unlike those of the cat, are non-retractable. The females have a 63-day gestation period. They give birth to fairly large litters, and the eyes of their young are closed at birth. It is also significant that members of these groups live in packs and respect a pack leader. This fact would explain why the domestic dog readily accepts the dictates of a human owner. The owner has become a substitute pack leader!

DOGDOM BC

The earliest identifiable remains of a pure-bred dog are those of a Saluki, a breed which took its name from the town of Saluk in the Yemen. Recent excavations of the Sumerian civilization in Mesopotamia, dated to 7000 BC, revealed rock carvings of dogs bearing a strong resemblance to the Saluki, the original ancestor of which is thought to have been a small-skulled desert wolf. The earliest domesticated dog in recorded history is the Pharaoh Hound: two hounds hunting gazelle are depicted on a circular disc dating back to around 4000 BC. The elegant and graceful Pharaoh Hound is known to have played an integral part in the daily lives of the kings of ancient Egypt.

However, while hounds such as the Saluki and Pharaoh lay claim to being the oldest pure-bred dogs on earth, it is interesting (bearing it in mind that wolves, jackals and dogs will interbreed under certain conditions) to detect those dogs that still resemble their ancestral equivalents and which have developed according not only to climatic conditions but also to the requirements of their new-found human friends.

Fox

Wolf

Saluki

WHO DOMESTICATED THE DOG?

IT IS LIKELY that prehistoric people, realizing they had nothing to fear from the dogs that crept towards their cave or camp fire seeking food and warmth, threw them some scraps of meat. The dogs, realizing, in turn, that humans were not predators, would have crept closer until a bond of companionship and mutual affection developed.

As time went on, humans would have recognized the value of the dog as a guard, beast of burden, sled dog and hunter, and later would have made the first crude attempts at selective breeding in a desire to perpetuate those traits of conformation, temperament and ability which they most admired.

Dogs, as we have seen, are descendants of the wolf and it is still possible today to see the result of some of the early attempts at selective breeding. Eskimo dogs are by no means dissimilar to the northern races of the wolf. They were frequently crossed with wolves to maintain their size and

DOGGY BONES

In 1979, Israeli archaeologists digging in the Middle East found the remains of a man and a puppy in close proximity. The hand of the man was resting on the puppy. This was among the remains of a 10,000-year-old Natufian settlement!

Above *The Samoyed takes its name from the Siberian tribe of Samoyedes. A descendant of the Siberian Wild Dog it nonetheless "shows affection for all mankind". The explorer Nansen took a number of "Sammies" with him on his expedition to the North Pole. In its native land it guards and protects reindeer.*

Left *Despite being reared by a human family, on reaching 2 or 3 years of age the Dingo's instinct to live with its own kind becomes stronger than the desire to remain with humans. Some believe it descends from Phu Quoc dogs of eastern Asia that were brought to Australia by seafarers.*

stamina. The Samoyed is a descendant of the Siberian Wild Dog. Dogs owned by the North American Indians tend to be smaller animals – likely descendants of the coyote or prairie wolf. Of all European dogs, the German Shepherd is certainly the most wolf-like. It was once known as the Alsatian Wolf Dog. Similarities such as these are readily found all over the world. Pariah dogs of India resemble the Indian wolf. Dogs in Africa, Asia and some parts of south-eastern Europe resemble the jackals of those regions, and the Australian dingo also resembles the jackal.

EARLY MAN'S BEST FRIEND

It is apparent that in the early days of domestication, and despite the friendship that had developed between humans and dogs, little or no effort was made to produce other than "useful" breeds. The written history of domesticated dogs is, for a thousand years, starting with a work by Xenophon (*c*430–*c*350 BC), essentially about hunting and hunting dogs. Indeed, it was not until 1685, in Nuremberg, that the first encyclopedia of dogs was published: the *Cynographia Curiosa oder Hundebeschreibung*, by Christian Franz Paullini.

A glimpse, however, of the changing role of the dog to meet social requirements, fashion and fancy, can be detected in a letter penned in 1560 by the Cambridge scholar, John Caius, to the Swiss naturalist, Gesner, in which he outlined the breeds of dog in England at that time:

"And we also have a small race of dogs that are specially bred to be the playthings of rich and noble ladies. The smaller they are, the more perfectly suited to their purpose, which is to be carried at the breast, in the bedchamber or in the lap, when their mistresses sally forth."

Hunting and watch dogs still predominated, but the lap dog had begun to make its mark.

DOG CENSUS

The domestic dog population of the world is estimated to be 150 million. America has the largest dog population, approximately 40 million. Britain has five and a half million. But these figures are not all for pure-bred dogs, and account for two and a half million mongrels.

A PACT

The dog is a creature that humans have never had to subdue into subservience, or with which they have been forced to do battle, for there are no ancient rock carvings illustrating such situations. It appears that Dog formed an alliance with Human of its own free will, and a partnership was formed on the basis of mutual friendship and trust.

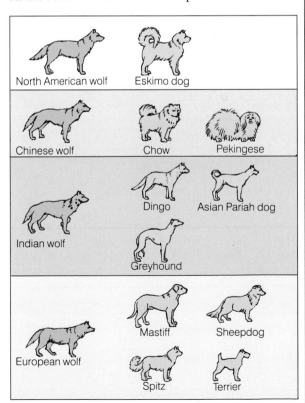

North American wolf · Eskimo dog

Chinese wolf · Chow · Pekingese

Indian wolf · Dingo · Asian Pariah dog · Greyhound

European wolf · Mastiff · Sheepdog · Spitz · Terrier

OLDEST BREEDS

● *The oldest pure-bred British dog is reckoned to be the Cardigan Welsh Corgi which traces back to dogs brought to Wales by the Celts from the Black Sea area around 1200 BC.*
● *The oldest pure-bred American breed is the American Foxhound. This dates back to 1650 when Robert Brooke, an Englishman, settled in Maryland, with his pack of foxhounds. These he crossed with other strains imported from England, Ireland and France, and thus the American Foxhound was developed.*

Were Dogs Always Popular?

THERE HAVE ALWAYS BEEN dog lovers and dog haters. Indeed, the recent rebellion in the United Kingdom against the proposed registration of dogs is nothing new. In 1796 there was a motion to introduce the first duties on dogs in England, five shillings on "outdoor" dogs, three shillings on "indoor" dogs. It was proposed by one George T. Clark, who was rewarded for his trouble with the receipt of dozens of dead dogs in hampers, packed as game. There was a massacre of dogs by owners who objected to paying the dues.

On balance the dog has been more revered than reviled through the ages. The ancient Egyptians are known to have had faithful dogs buried alongside them, a practice also followed in ancient America by the Toltec people, and later by the Aztecs, whose dogs were sacrificed at funerals in the belief that they would guide their masters to a better world.

HOLY DOGS

We know that the dog has played a large part in Eastern religions and that although it is considered by Moslems to be an outcast of Allah, and unclean,

Status Dogs

● *Wealth and snobbery have always played their part in dog ownership and, in the time of King Richard I of England, anyone who kept a greyhound, unless he was worth ten pounds a year in land or inheritance, or 300 pounds a year in freehold, was liable to be summoned to the Forest Court, which met every year to determine whether his greyhound had been running in the forest.*
● *In the Middle Ages there were reckoned to be no less than 69 Royal Forests, 800 Parks and 13 Chases in England and the comment was frequently made that, if you wanted to see a King of England you need look no further than the hunting field.*
● *The common people were allowed to keep only watch dogs and small dogs which were incapable of bringing down game and therefore spoiling their betters' sport. Large dogs would be systematically and cruelly lamed.*
● *To this day there exists in the village of Lyndhurst in the County of Hampshire a measure, or stirrup, through which a dog had to pass so as to assess whether it was sufficiently small to be allowed to roam unhindered in the forest.*

the fleet-footed Saluki is still prized along with pure-bred Arab horses.

Hindus believe that a person who ill-treats a dog will be punished by returning to earth in canine form. It is often the fear of the unknown that has made humans behave unreasonably towards animals. Here lies the source of Totemism – the identification of themselves by human families with an animal family – and of Metempsychosis – the belief in the transmigration of human souls, and their return in an animal's body.

The importance of shepherd dogs and guard

Left While in the East Moslems scorned the dog, credited with devouring the body of the Prophet, Mohammed, fear of the animal was also prevalent in Europe, where the word dog, or 'cur' became an insult.

Above The Saluki is a fleet-footed dog able to keep pace with fast Arab horses. In the Middle East it is still used for hunting the gazelle. Elsewhere it is mainly kept as a lean and elegant pet.

STARRY DOG

Even in astrology, dogs are a force to be reckoned with and there is more than a little truth in the saying that, "every dog has its day". There are forty "dog days" between 3 July and 11 August, when Sirius, the Dog Star, rises and sets with the sun. The superstition that Sirius greatly influences the canine race is found in Greek literature, as far back as Hesiod in the eighth century BC.

dogs was stressed in the teachings of the Persian prophet, Zoroaster (Zarathustra), almost three thousand years ago. Zoroaster's doctrine, which spread widely in the East, bore many references to dogs and their importance. He decreed: "If these two dogs of mine, the shepherd dog and the guard dog, pass the house of any of my faithful people, let them never be kept away from it, for no house could exist, but for these two dogs of mine, the shepherd dog and guard dog."

Dogs were even worshipped by the followers of Mithras, who was aided and accompanied by his dog, and whose cult flourished for almost five centuries in Roman times, spreading from India to Spain and from Egypt to the south of Scotland.

There is a dog-worshipping sect to this day. It is called the Brotherhood of the Essenes. The Essenes maintain that there are animal planes in the celestial Kingdom from which one steps to the planes of knowledge. It is their view that animals have power of speech in the Kingdom which they relinquish voluntarily as they journey through the gates of the zodiac into earth's sphere. According to their beliefs, dogs are beings without sin, sent to earth to test humans.

HAVE ANY BREEDS DISAPPEARED?

MANY DOGS HAVE DISAPPEARED – some (like the unfortunate "turnspit") into total extinction, others being sacrificed in the development of another or changed variety.

The "turnspit" is, in the words of canine historian, Carson Ritchie, "the best known representative of those worker-dogs which had once provided power for various purposes, such as raising water from a well by working a treadmill."

Prior to the introduction of the "turnspit" dog, meat in 18th century England was turned on the spit by a human, usually a small boy, protected by the fierce heat with a round, woven, straw shield, soaked in water. However, special treadmills were built near to the fires of large kitchens in great houses and dogs were trained to keep them turning. It would take at least three hours for a large side of beef to roast properly. The dog had to turn the wheel hundreds of times and was subject to beatings from the cook if it paused in its unenviable task. So exhausting was the work that sometimes two "turnspit" dogs were kept, so that one might

Right *The Bulldog is the breed most generally associated with bull-baiting. It would seize the bull by the nose and hold it until it fell. This unsavoury sport was promoted by an Englishman, Earl Warren of Stamford. After watching two dogs fight bulls in 1209 he sought to bring the spectacle to a wider audience. It was made illegal in 1838.*

Below *"Cave Canem": Beware the dog. In Ancient Rome fierce dogs were highly prized, though rarely for their fidelity. They were watchdogs, messengers and combatants. Sometimes they would be starved before meeting their opponents.*

THE QUEEN'S POM

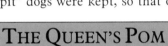

Queen Victoria, an avid lover of most breeds of dogs, became a champion of the Toy varieties, notably, and before the arrival in England of the Pekingese, of the Pomeranian, which initially was a much larger dog weighing as much as 13.5kg (30lb). The Pomeranian was however bred down and by 1896 show classes for the breed had been divided into those for exhibits under and over 3.5kg (8lb) in weight. By 1915 exhibits over that weight had all but disappeared.

work on the other's day off.

What did the "turnspit" dog look like? It has been described as:

"extremely bandy legged, so as to appear almost incapable of running, with long bodies and rather large heads. They are very strong in the jaws, and are what are called 'hard bitten'. It is a peculiarity in these dogs that they generally have the iris of one eye black, and the other white. Their colour varies, but the usual one is a blueish-grey, spotted with black. The tail is generally curled on the back."

At any rate, this sadly misused little animal was to survive until around 1870, by which time it had become so rare that owners of such treasures were enabled to hire them out by the day.

There were also, up until the 19th century, dogs such as the cur, a cross between sheepdog and terrier, and the drover's dog, a cross between a sheepdog and mastiff, the task of which was to guide a farmer's sheep to market. The cur was a watchdog with perhaps less than the social standing of the present day mongrel, and its title had become a derogatory term.

RARE AND UNUSUAL DOGS

AS I WRITE, the world's rarest dog is reckoned to be the Tahltan bear dog which, as its name implies, was once used by the Tahltan Indians of western Canada for bear hunting, also against lynx and porcupine. It is understood that the Indians carried these dogs – the weight of which is around 13kg (30lb) – in hide sacks on their backs, so as to preserve their strength for when the quarry was sighted, at which time they would promptly be released. The job of the bear dog was to hold the proposed victim at bay, circling it until its masters moved in for the kill. There must be less than a handful of the breed now alive and it is sadly in danger of extinction. This was a fate which threatened the Chinese Shar Pei and the Chinese Crested dog not so long ago, and both are now fairly commonplace, particularly in the British show ring.

THE PODENGO

It would indeed be true to say that what is rare today may not be rare tomorrow, so one must hope that the future will be brighter for another breed threatened with extinction, the Portuguese Warren

Right The Portuguese Warren Hound (Pequeno) is usually fawn, but may be yellow, brown, grey-black or sooty, with or without white patches and spots. It is not currently recognized by the American and United Kingdom Kennel Clubs or the International Canine Federation (FCI).

ON ICE

The Broholmer is a breed recognized only in its native Denmark. It was believed to have become extinct in the 1960s but then, in December 1974, a dog of the breed appeared at the home of a pharmacist in Helsinki, Finland. The Royal Veterinary College in Copenhagen set up a frozen sperm bank for the dog, which was named Bjoern, in the hope that a bitch might eventually be found. But alas, this did not prove to be the case, and Bjoern died in January 1975.

A ROCK DAY

The Lundehund is a breed which for centuries has lived solely on two islands in the north of Norway. Unlike other dogs which have four toes, possibly an atrophied fifth, the Lundehund has five toes and an atrophied sixth. Also, unlike other small dogs with five toe cushions, the Lundehund has seven or eight. Because of its small size and this strange foot equipment the dog is enabled to scale rocks and cliffs so as to gently lift a Puffin from its nest and restore it unharmed to his master.

COURT FAVOURITES

It is recorded by the famous diarist, Samuel Pepys, that King Charles II spent more time playing with his dogs in the Council Chamber than he did on affairs of state. However, credited as the most fanatical dog lover of all time was Henry III of France (1551–89). Indeed, according to the Guinness Book of Pet Records *he collected dogs as people collect stamps. When he saw one that took his fancy, and it wasn't for sale, he would think nothing of arranging for someone to steal it for him. Seemingly he had at least 2000 dogs spread around his palaces and, when he was in residence, there were never less than 100 dogs, mostly toy breeds, within patting distance. But then the love of Royalty for dogs is well known. Edward VII's faithful Fox Terrier, "Caesar", followed his late master's funeral procession, and "Slipper", a Cairn Terrier given by Edward VIII to the then Mrs. Wallis Simpson, featured largely in their much publicised courtship correspondence. The present Queen, Elizabeth II, is rarely photographed in home surroundings without a few Corgi dogs beside her.*

Left The Portuguese Water Dog is a very muscular animal. Its toes are webbed to their tips with a soft membrane covered with hair. It may be black, white or various shades of brown; or combinations of black or brown with white.

Hound, or Podengo, which is little known outside its country of origin where it is a hunter of rabbit, hare and deer. There are three sizes of this variety, the *grande* (large), which stands 56–68cm (22–27in) high, and whose numbers are diminishing, a small variety *(pequeno)*, which resembles a large, smooth-coated Chihuahua, and a medium sized dog. The *grande* is not unlike the Ibizan Hound.

THE PORTUGUESE WATER DOG

There is another Portuguese dog which is unusual albeit not so rare, and that is the Portuguese water dog, a fascinating animal, which was once readily to be seen at Portuguese and Spanish seaports working as a fisherman's dog, guarding his nets. It is remarkable in that it will catch an escaping fish in its jaws and swim back with it to its master. There are short, curly-coated and long-coated varieties, but it is the latter that calls for attention when it is presented in a smart lion clip similar to that of the elegant standard Poodle.

THE LOWCHEN

The Lowchen, a native French breed, registered in its country of origin under the title, "petit chien lion", little lion dog, had all but died out little more than 20 years ago, but is now a popular contender in the show ring – though little seen, it must be admitted, being taken for a walk in a park. Believed to have been a favourite of the Duchess of Alba, it is thought that the dog shown with her in a portrait painted by Francisco Goya (1746–1828) is a Lowchen. There is no doubt about the breed in the delightful portrait, *A Lowchen Seated by a Quill* painted by Florent-Richard De Lamarre between 1630 and 1718, revealing, then as now, the distinctive lion clip which is worn by this delightful member of the Bichon family.

WHAT IS A PURE BREED?

A PURE-BRED DOG is one whose sire (father) and dam (mother) are of the same breed, the parents having themselves descended from dogs of the same breed. It has been explained how early people would have attempted planned matings of their canine companions so as to perpetuate those traits they admired and desired. They would have experimented with such things as height, weight, and coat-type, with colour patterns, with the shape of the dog's head and skull, and the setting of its tail until, in the course of a few generations the desired canine type would breed true.

Doubtless subsequent dog fanciers would have discussed the attributes of their animals much as people do today. However, while we have the legacy of many paintings which depict breeds of dogs that appear to have changed little from those we know now, it is almost impossible to chart their progress. This is because it was not until 1873 that the Kennel Club in London – the first of its kind in the world – was formed. The Kennel Club introduced a registration system, so that one might determine the breeding of every pure-bred canine – in what amounted to its own birth certificate – and also refer to an approved "Standard" for each variety of dog that was recognized.

Of course the desire to continue to introduce and improve breeds has continued and there are remarkably few varieties which do not owe their present existence to another breed. The Doberman, for example, owes much to the Rottweiler and Manchester Terrier, and the little Long Coat Chihuahua to the Papillon, or Butterfly dog, so named because of the shape of its ears.

TALLEST AND SHORTEST

- *The tallest dog breeds are the Great Dane, the Irish wolfhound, the St. Bernard, the English mastiff, the Borzoi and the Anatolian Karabash (Turkish Shepherd dog). All of these breeds can attain 90 cm (36 in) at the shoulder.*
- *The smallest dog breed is the Chihuahua, the recognized weight of which is between 0.9–2.75kg (two and six pounds). Mexico City's natural history museum, however, has the skeleton of a fully grown Chihuahua measuring only 18cm (seven in) in total length. There is no weight quoted for this dog, which was presented in 1910, but it is estimated that, if its bones are anything to go by, it could not have weighed more than one pound.*
- *The second smallest dog is reckoned to be the Yorkshire Terrier which "officially" should not weigh more than 3.20kg (seven pounds), but many pet "Yorkies" nowadays tend to be much heavier.*

Right *The Greyhound is a pure breed that has not altered materially from its likeness carved in an Egyptian tomb in the Nile Valley c. 4000 BC. It has been used for coursing since Roman times. Nowadays it is bred along distinct lines for showing, coursing and track racing.*

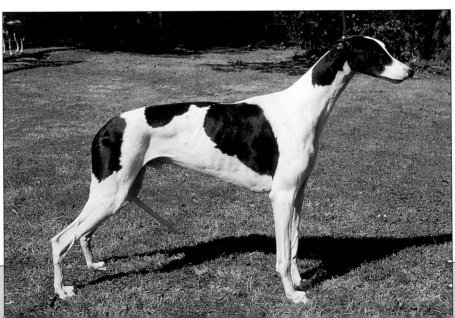

WHAT ARE CROSSBREEDS?

A CROSSBREED is the progeny of a pure-bred bitch which has mated with a pure-bred dog of another pure breed – for example, the result of a Poodle–Spaniel mating.

There are those who favour a crossbreed believing that they will have the benefit of the attributes of both breeds. In fact, a problem often arises where an owner, having lost a crossbreed of a certain type wishes to replace it with another, for crossbreeds are rarely intentionally bred.

A mongrel is a dog or bitch whose sire and dam are likely to owe their make-up to any number of different breeds.

OLD WIVES' TALE

There is an old wives' tale that mongrels are more robust than pure-bred dogs. In fact, the mongrel is unlikely to be any tougher, or weaker, than its pure-bred contemporaries.

There is no doubt that Mongrels make excellent pets but there is always an element of uncertainty as to how they will turn out in regard to either appearance or temperament.

pure breed of same type = pure breed

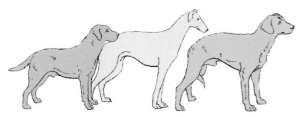

pure breeds of different type = "X" breed

"X" breed + "X" breed = mongrel

Above Mongrels come in all shapes and sizes. This example could well have a touch of Boxer in its makeup. White Boxers do sometimes occur, but are not accepted in the show ring. They do, however, make excellent pets.

Right Mongrels have tremendous appeal. Whereas with a pure-bred pup you can be reasonably sure how it will turn out, with a mongrel you have to take pot luck.

Left The result of mating two pure-bred dogs of different breeds can be successful or somewhat startling, depending on the varieties involved.

FEET FIRST

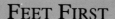

The best way to determine how large a mongrel puppy is likely to grow is to look at the size of its feet. A pup with really large feet is destined to be a mammoth-sized dog.

WHAT IS A CERTIFICATE OF PEDIGREE?

IT IS A COMMON mistake to refer to a "pedigree" dog. The correct term is a pure-bred dog. A Certificate of Pedigree is the document which should be handed to the buyer of a pure-bred pup at the time of purchase. The buyer should also be given a Transfer form enabling him or her, for a modest fee, to register the pup in the buyer's name, in place of the vendor's, with the respective national kennel club.

The Certificate of Pedigree which, like the Transfer form, should be signed by the breeder, must show the registered name and number of the puppy – obviously you can call your pup whatever pet name you wish – its date of birth, and the registered names and registration numbers of its parents and ancestors for three, or preferably five, generations.

This Certificate of Pedigree is a valuable document which calls for careful scrutiny. Unless the pup's parents are registered, and the signature of the breeder appears, the new owner will be unable to register a transfer of ownership and, perhaps more importantly, will be unable to enter the dog in pure-breed show classes, or to register and sell its subsequent progeny as pure-bred.

You will probably notice on a Certificate of Pedigree, that most of the dogs' names bear a Prefix, for instance, Merry Max of Penfold, or Penfold Merry Max. This is because breeders, again for a modest fee, are enabled to register a Prefix with their respective kennel club, which enables stock from their kennels to be easily recognized. Where a dog has been bred by the Prefix holder, the word will appear in front of the dog's name (called an Affix). If the dog has been acquired, the Prefix will follow the dog's name, for example "of" or "at", and this is called a Suffix.

HOW TO DETECT PRIZE-WINNING STOCK

If you attend dog shows and look at the catalogue entries for a specific breed, you may find it interesting to detect, from their affixes, those kennels that predominate and produce considerable prize-winning stock.

Below *The points of the dog. It is necessary to know the points of the dog to fully understand the breed Standard as set by the Kennel Clubs, the breed Standard being the definitive of what each breed type should conform to.*

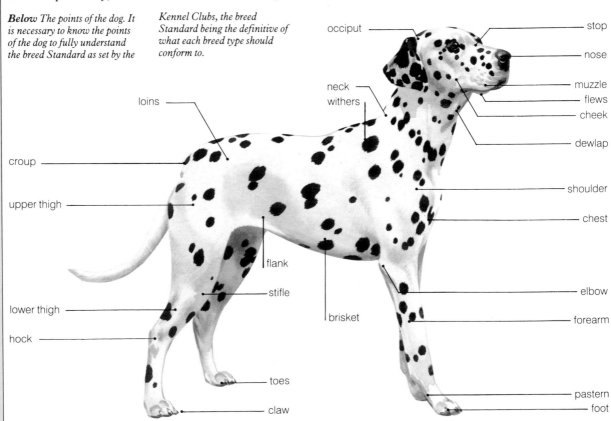

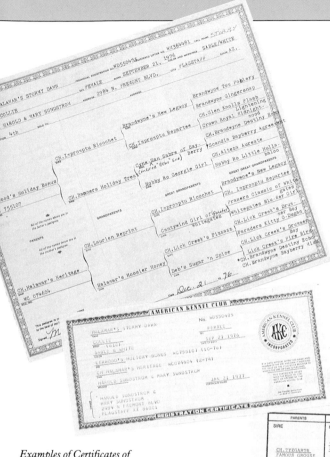

Pedigree certificates are usually completed by hand. Those which have entries written in red ink are highly prized, for only the names of champions are thus honoured.

The American and British championship systems are different. In Britain, champions are dogs which have been awarded three Challenge Certificates at three different Championship Dog Shows and by three different judges. In the USA, a championship is attained via an accumulation of points. A dog that has accumulated 15 points is designated a Champion. The dog may earn from one to five points at a show, and only one male and one female can win points a show.

It is worth repeating that, when buying a pup, the Certificate of Pedigree warrants careful scrutiny and that even if the pup you intend to buy is an attractive and healthy example of its breed, and you have no intention of exhibiting or breeding from it, if the Certificate is incomplete, the pup should not command as high a price as its fellows which are correctly documented.

*Examples of Certificates of Pedigree and registration documents: **Top** US Pedigree; **Above** American Kennel Club Registration Certificate; **Right** UK Pedigree; **Below right** The UK Kennel Club Registration Certificate.*

CHAMPION OF CHAMPIONS

The greatest number of Challenge Certificates, or "CCs" as fanciers call them, to be won by a British dog, were the 78 awarded to Champion (Ch) U'Kwong King Solomon, a Chow Chow owned and bred by Mrs. Joan Egerton of Bramhall, Cheshire in the north of England. Known as Solly, this magnificent Chow Chow died in 1978 aged 10 years. It is the life's ambition of some dog exhibitors to win even one Challenge Certificate.

ARE PEDIGREE DOGS SHOW DOGS?

THE ACQUISITION OF A CERTIFICATE of Pedigree proves that you own a pure-bred dog. It enables you to register ownership with the national kennel club, to legitimately enter the animal in pure-bred show classes and, if you wish to breed, to sell its progeny with a similar Certificate of Pedigree. But – contrary to a widely held belief – a pedigreed dog is by no means always a prospect for the show ring.

FALLING SHORT OF PERFECTION

Kennel clubs worldwide have what is known as a *Standard* laid down for each recognized breed. This Standard describes the perfect example of every variety and it is the dogs which meet this exacting requirement that compete against each other in the show ring. There are however countless breed members which fall short of their Standard of perfection, if only in some minor detail – they may be slightly too big, or too small, their teeth formation may be under or over-shot, or there could be a wrongful patch of colour on their coats – in which case, they would be sold (most pure-bred dogs are) as "pet" dogs rather than show dogs.

Most people only want an attractive, faithful companion of their favourite breed. However, problems can arise when, having made a purchase, and thinking that their pet is a show dog, they enter

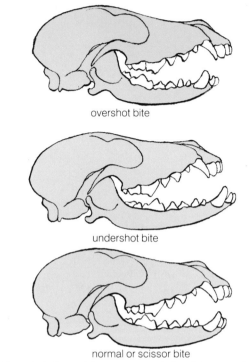

overshot bite

undershot bite

normal or scissor bite

Above A dog's mouth is overshot when the upper teeth project beyond the lower. It is undershot if the lower jaw projects.

Below The correct shape and position of the tail varies according to the breed.

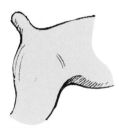

set high and carried erect (usually docked)

ring tail, set high

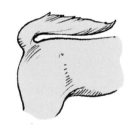

set high, folded along the back

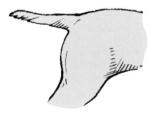

set high and carried horizontally, low in repose

long, set high and carried sickle-like, low in repose

medium set-on, carried sabre-like

otter tail of medium length, rounded without feather

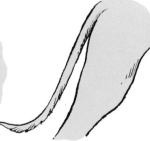

long, set low and curved at the tip

erect ears with medium-high set-on (sometimes cropped)

bat ears, set high and broad at the base

pendulous ears, set low

folded ears, drooping forward

rose ears, set back

semi-erect ears

it in a show with disastrous results. "But my dog has a Certificate of Pedigree," they then say. "I paid a good price for it. I have been swindled if my dog is not a show dog." But the truth of the matter is that they have been treated fairly having bought a healthy example of the breed. They never asked the breeder for a show dog.

Obtaining a show prospect is not easy, particularly as it is rarely possible to determine a dog's true potential until it is six months of age, or more. Often breeders will "run-on" a likely pup in their kennels, with a view to exhibiting and/or breeding from it themselves. A good dog is an advertisement for their kennels!

Those who want to exhibit must first convince a breeder that they will prove to be a worthy owner, and of their keenness to become involved in the breed, probably by joining the relevant Breed Club, attending many shows as a spectator and learning all they can about handling the variety. Once they have passed this test, and been rewarded with the acquisition of their first show dog, they will discover that the World of Show Dogs is a completely new way of life.

Left *The size, position and fall of the ears is also specified in the breed Standard.*

Below *The Dalmatian's spots should be clearly defined. Those on the extremities should be smaller than those on the body.*

THE SUPREME SHOW

Crufts Dog Show is the largest dog show in the world. It has been held annually in London since 1886, with the exception of the years 1918–20 and 1940–47, when it was cancelled. When the show was first held at the Royal Aquarium in Westminster, it was restricted to terrier breeds, but four years later, other breeds, including Toys, were added. The Golden Jubilee show held at the Royal Agricultural Hall, Islington, in 1936, attracted record numbers, 10,650 entries and 4388 dogs. However this was before entry was restricted, as is now the case, to prizewinners in Championship Shows. The British Kennel Club has run Crufts since 1948, the venue being London's Olympia Halls and subsequently Earls Court Exhibition Centre. However, in January 1991, the show moved to the National Exhibition Centre in Birmingham to celebrate its Centenary.

ARE DOGS INTELLIGENT?

Left: These curious Jack Russell pups enjoying tug of war are having a dress rehearsal for the more serious business of hunting rats and other small vermin.

THIS IS A QUESTION which scientists have argued over for centuries. We know that dogs are incapable of logical thought as we know it. They cannot reason as we can, but in terms of a "domestic wolf" they are indeed intelligent, relying on association, scent, instinct and memory. They also display characteristics of guarding, loyalty and playfulness which are typical of the wolf pack and, I would add, a keen sense of humour.

It is known that pups, untouched by human hands during the first weeks of life, never become wholly domesticated. Similarly, the dog that is kennelled, fed, groomed and exercised, but otherwise given little attention, is unlikely to reach the same potential as its contemporary which is kept as a household pet, spoken to regularly, played with and introduced to any number of outside influences and experiences.

TEACHING YOUR DOG

Dog training must be interpreted by the dog as an extension of play. Learning, however, is largely a matter of association. Some dogs, like some humans, are more intelligent than others, but there are few, given time, which, having recognized the key words, will not react to sentences such as: "Shall we (Let's) go for a WALK, Ben", "Goodness, it's time for BED, Ben!", "Do you want your DINNER?", "Here's MUM (or Dad)!" and "Let's go and meet JANE". The list is endless and the dog's reaction could reasonably be thought to mean that it understands the meaning of the word spoken. It cannot do so, but associates the key word, whether or not used in conjunction with its name, with the action that takes place thereafter.

ACTIONS RATHER THAN WORDS

It is not just the spoken word that brings about this association in the canine mind. Actions can speak as loudly as words. The mere fact of a dog's owner walking into the hall, or kitchen, with a coat on may be enough for the dog to jump up from its basket in anticipation of a walk, while the sound of a car engine in the drive may be sufficient to send it running hurriedly to the door in anticipation of its master's arrival. Undoubtedly the more time one spends with one's dog the more it learns, and the more it learns, the more it endears itself to us.

Most pet owners have only one dog. They do not have the same opportunity, as those who keep several, of studying the behaviour of the social pack.

SUBSTITUTE PACK LEADERS

It has been explained how humans became substitute pack leaders, whom our domesticated wolf knows he must respect. Where, however, there are a number of dogs, the biggest, strongest male will generally emerge as the canine pack leader. He will marshal his troops, standing aside, for instance, until all have been accounted for when going out of doors. He will guard the food bowls, sometimes literally forbidding another dog to eat until he allows it to do so – even, on some occasions, giving an unliked subordinate what amounts to the evil eye until the unfortunate animal creeps away into a corner. Much however depends on the breed and temperament of the dog.

Often there is a second in command, even a third in pecking order, while some dogs do not aspire to leadership at all. Disagreements are rare except where three important factors raise their head: sex, food and jealousy.

Above In a domestic situation the dog regards its human owner as a substitute pack leader. It feels secure in the subordinate role and wants only to win the leader's approval.

MOOD MONITORS

- *One of the reasons why dogs bring great comfort to humans is their uncanny facility of picking up our moods. The dog, in common with its ancestor, the wolf, is sensitive to atmosphere. That is why it will come and sit quietly beside us when we are despondent or jump around enthusiastically when we are in high spirits.*
- *Dogs have an inbuilt sense of time. How else would they know to draw attention to themselves when a regular feeding time draws near?*
- *It has also been proved that dogs can recognize places, even if they have not visited them for months, or even years. Indeed, a dog that has been sleeping quietly in the back of a car may get up and show considerable excitement within a kilometre or so of a once familiar location.*

CAN DOGS PERFORM USEFUL TASKS?

IT IS ALMOST impossible to list the many useful tasks which dogs undertake, but I will endeavour to mention a few.

There are Search and Rescue Dogs, specially trained to detect missing persons or bodies in an area of scent. They are highly trained dogs, which frequently live the life of family pets when not on call. The dogs go out, with their masters, usually skilful hill climbers, in all weathers, and their value is being increasingly recognized in the case of avalanches, aircraft crashes and earthquakes.

ARMED SERVICE DOGS

There are dogs in the Armed Services, working for Customs and Excise and for the Police. They are variously used as Guards, Patrol Dogs, and as "Sniffer" Dogs trained in the detection of explosives and narcotics. Some dogs, particularly the Bloodhound, with its incredible scenting ability, are used to track criminals or find lost children.

DOGS THAT "SEE" AND "HEAR"

Perhaps the best known worker dogs are Sheepdogs and Guide Dogs for the Blind. However there are also Hearing Dogs for the Deaf. A "hearing" dog is taught to respond to the sounds chosen by the individual applicant like a knock at the door, the whistle of a kettle, or the ring of a telephone or alarm clock, happenings that would go undetected by the deaf person were it not for the help of their dog in drawing attention to them.

IT SEEMS LIKE PLAY

Work must always be interpreted by a dog as play. When an RAF Sniffer dog is being trained, his reward is to retrieve. When a young dog retrieves a package of cannabis he will be allowed to have a game with the package, but that will be the only game he is allowed when working.

A dog's instincts are channelled into retrieving a particular scent. The dog gets every individual scent and breaks it down in its head until it finds the one that it knows its master desires, regardless of what else is with it. The dog builds up a "scent picture". Every picture given to the dog includes the drug or explosive that the dog has been trained to find as a common denominator.

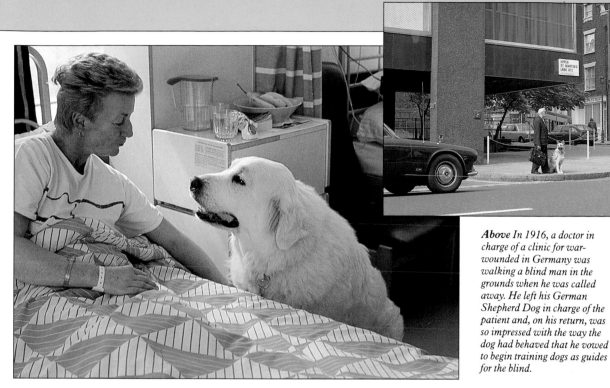

Above In 1916, a doctor in charge of a clinic for war-wounded in Germany was walking a blind man in the grounds when he was called away. He left his German Shepherd Dog in charge of the patient and, on his return, was so impressed with the way the dog had behaved that he vowed to begin training dogs as guides for the blind.

Far left Sniffer dogs are on active service in many countries.

Left "Hearing Dogs for the Deaf" have proved so successful that dogs are being trained for other disabilities.

Above Dogs are always needed to join the Pro Dogs Active Therapy team, but first they must pass a rigorous temperament test. Some top show-dogs are on the register, as are crossbreeds and mongrels.

DR. DOG

One of the proudest chapters in sled dog history was written in 1925. It was in January of that year that a case of diptheria was discovered in Nome, Alaska. The supply of antitoxin in that city was insufficient to ward off an epidemic. A relay of 22 native and mail teams forged through the rough interior of Alaska and across the Bering Sea ice to bring the serum to the grateful citizens. Today in Central Park, New York, stands a statue of Balto who led one of the relay teams commemorating the Nome Serum Run. An inscription reads: Dedicated to the indomitable spirit of the sled dogs that relayed antitoxin 600 miles over rough ice, treacherous waters, through arctic blizzards from Nemana to the relief of stricken Nome in the winter of 1925. Endurance, Fidelity, Intelligence.

DOGS FOR PETTING

There are Assistance Dogs for the Disabled also trained to answer their special needs, and Pro-Dogs Active Therapy Dogs which, with their owners, visit hospitals, nursing homes and hospices, brightening the lives of those persons who may no longer be able to keep a dog of their own. Indeed it has been proved that the mere act of stroking a dog can help to reduce a patient's blood pressure .

The presence of dogs is being increasingly recognized as therapy and canines are finding their way, as residents, into a growing number of psychiatric and geriatric hospitals and hospices.

In the United Kingdom it is not permitted to allow a dog to pull a cart on a public highway. But in America it is not unusual for a large dog to bring home the groceries in this fashion, while in Switzerland the Bernese Mountain Dog may be seen drawing a milk churn. In its native Germany the Rottweiler was traditionally the butcher's dog.

Dogs do of course appear in films, television commercials and on the live stage. But perhaps their most important task of all is as companion to the lonely and elderly, those people who would have nobody to relate to were it not for their faithful friend, the dog.

CAN DOGS LOVE?

THE PROVERB SAYS, "A dog never bites the hand that feeds it", and cynics may say that as dogs rely on us for their creature comfort, any show of affection is self motivated – it wishes to safeguard its meal ticket. There have, however, been far too many true stories illustrating the unselfish love of dogs for their masters for such arguments to carry much weight.

It must be admitted that dogs thrive best, and are happiest, when their routine is undisturbed. Like humans they become attuned to sleeping on a familiar bed, or basket, eating their dinner and going out for walks at regular hours. A break in routine when, for example, the family member who usually exercises the dog goes away, or it is put into boarding kennels, can account for loss of condition.

But there is no doubt that dogs, particularly those which live in close proximity with their owners, often sharing the same sleeping quarters, and rarely leaving their side, can literally pine to death should their owner predecease them.

THE STORY OF GREYFRIARS BOBBY

In my view, it is the true story of Greyfriars Bobby which best illustrates the lasting love of a dog for its master. Bobby was a small, shaggy terrier, possibly a Skye terrier, the much loved companion of a Midlothian farmer named Gray.

Each Wednesday, Bobby would accompany his master to market in Edinburgh and, at mid-day or thereafter, the two would repair to Traill's tearooms where Gray had his mid-day meal and Bobby would be given a bun. In 1858 Gray died, and was laid to rest in Greyfriars Churchyard.

On the third day following the funeral, at the usual time of Gray's visit, Bobby, bedraggled and looking the picture of woe, presented himself at the tea-rooms where, out of pity, Traill gave the dog its customary bun.

It was thought that this would be the last that those at the tearooms would see of Bobby. But the next day and the day after, the dog appeared and again was given, and trotted off with, its bun.

Finally, his curiosity aroused, Traill decided to follow Bobby. This he did, and was surprised to find the little dog heading for Greyfriars Churchyard. When the dog got there it lay down on its master's grave and ate its scanty lunch.

It soon became evident that Gray had been a loner and that no provision had been made for Bobby; also that the little dog was spending its days and nights lying on the grave, leaving its vigil only

Below Dogs enjoy human companionship. They like to be close to their owners, and often enjoy accompanying them during routine daily activities.

TREKKER SETTER

Some dogs love their home, almost as much as their master. In August 1976 an Irish (Red) Setter named Bede went missing while on holiday in Cornwall with his owner, Father Louis Heston. Almost six months later, Bede, footsore and weary, turned up at his master's home in Braintree, Essex, having travelled 480km (300 miles). The Kennel Club declared Bede the Bravest Dog of 1976 and he was presented with his award at Crufts Dog Show on 12 February 1977.

DOG POWER

In America, canine weight-hauling contests are very popular, competing dogs testing their strength and endurance by pulling heavy loads. The World Championship Weight Hauling Contest is held at Bothell, Washington, as part of the annual Northwest Newfoundland Club Working Dog Trials. There are five weight categories: under 45kg (100lb), 45–59kg (100–130lb), 59–75kg (130–165lb), 75–86kg (165–190lb) and over 86kg (190lb). However, the greatest recorded load to have been shifted by a dog was 2905kg (6400½lb) pulled by a 80kg (176lb) St. Bernard named Ryettes Brandy Bear at Bothell on 21 July 1978, on which occasion the other dogs entered, three Newfoundlands, two Alaskan Malamutes and another St. Bernard, also pulled 25 times their own body-weight on their first haul.

to go to the tearooms when forced to do so by pangs of hunger.

Normally, dogs were not allowed into Greyfriars Churchyard, but the rule was eventually waived in the case of Bobby who, taking refuge only in wet weather in a nearby shelter, provided by compassionate friends, and refusing any attempt at re-homing, continued his vigil for the next fourteen years until his death in 1872, when he was buried, like his master, in Greyfriars Churchyard.

Later, a statue in Bobby's likeness was erected by the people of Edinburgh to commemorate this little dog which, even following its master's death, could not be persuaded to leave his side.

Above Play is a good way to build up friendship and loyalty between owner and dog, as well as reinforcing training lessons.

Left Most dogs are keen to please their owners, and once trained they can be encouraged to carry out all kinds of tasks and activities.

WHERE CAN I GET A DOG?

ONCE YOU HAVE DECIDED whether you want a pure-bred, cross-bred or mongrel, you must make up your mind if you would like a dog or a bitch. This is entirely a matter of choice. Many people prefer bitches, believing them to be easier to train, and because of their gentler, maternal nature a better companion for children. Others welcome a dog's more zestful approach to life. However, it is worth mentioning that the woman who buys a bitch may find that it becomes more attached to her partner while the dog, intended as the man's companion, prefers the lady.

CHOOSING A DOG

Also to be considered is whether the dog is to be big or small and short- or long-coated, bearing in mind that the long coat will require extensive grooming and that even a short-coated breed, with a light coat will deposit noticeable hairs on the carpet.

Mongrels and crossbreeds can be obtained from pet shops, from the rescue kennels of animal welfare societies and through advertisements in local newspapers. You may even see pups advertised on post cards in shop windows. If you have not set your heart on a puppy, you could be doing a misplaced, older dog a favour by offering it a home. There are likely to be several to choose from at your local or breed rescue kennels.

SAFETY NET

● *Breed rescue societies have been set up by almost all breed societies in an effort to rehome misplaced members of their breed – dogs of various ages whose owners have had to relinquish them for a variety of reasons.*

● *Breed rescue offers an opportunity for those seeking a particular breed but reluctant, or unable, to take on a puppy, to obtain an older dog of their favourite breed. Obviously only genuine applications are considered and "rescue" should not be regarded as a cheap means of obtaining a pure-bred dog.*

If you want a pure-bred, much depends on whether you are looking for a pet or show dog, because the pure-bred dogs you see advertised in newspapers, or glimpse in pet shop windows, are unlikely to be destined for the show ring.

Once you have narrowed down your choice to one or two breeds, a call to your national kennel club will elicit details of reputable breeders. Bear in mind that, if you live in a city, it is unlikely that a breeder of, say, Mastiffs will live around the corner, so you must be prepared to travel some distance, and to have your name put on a waiting list.

Don't be put off if breeders ask lots of seaching

Character is formed early. Always choose an inquisitive confident pup. The timid one is likely to grow into a nervous dog.

Above The Wood Green Animal Shelter in England is one of the most modern in Europe. Records of every inmate are held on computer.

questions – whether you have a garden, for instance, and whether you have a job, or are at home all day. The mere fact of their doing so proves that they have the welfare of their stock at heart.

If you would like a pure-bred which is well past puppy stage, even five years of age or more, ask your national kennel club to let you have the address of the relevant breed rescue society. They might have a dog of the chosen breed needing rehoming for any number of reasons, ranging from the death of a previous owner to a marriage breakup.

Don't make a hasty decision about your choice of dog. After all, it is destined to be your companion for twelve years or maybe more.

Left You should make sure that the puppy of your choice is healthy before finalizing the purchase. 1. Pick up the puppy to check that it does not object or show signs of pain; its body should be firm and relaxed. 2. Lift the ear flap and check that the ear canal is dry and clean. 3. Open the mouth gently and check that the tongue and gums are pink. 4. The eyes should be clear and bright, and there should be no signs of discharge. 5. Run your hand against the grain of the coat to check for sores and the black dust caused by fleas. 6. Check under the tail that there is no staining, which would indicate diarhoea.

GETTING READY FOR YOUR NEW PET

THERE ARE ITEMS TO BE BOUGHT, and precautions to be taken, before your pup arrives.

First of all, make sure that your garden is adequately fenced. If it is not, arrange for the work to be carried out speedily, bearing in mind that gates and fencing must be flush with the ground, and that the foot of the netting must be buried to ensure tiny breeds cannot crawl underneath.

Experienced dog owners, lucky enough to have big gardens, often net or fence off an area specially for their pets. This enables them, particularly if they are keen gardeners, to safeguard the remaining area for horticulture. However, you may wish to confine your dog to a yard, which can be easily swilled down with a disinfectant solution. There are disposal units for canine excrement available from pet stores and hardware sources.

WHAT TO BUY

An indoor wire pen, with a plastic, removable floor tray, is an excellent investment, and can be obtained in various sizes. Into the pen will go the pup's basket, preferably of the polyurethane type

LEAD: YES – HARNESS: NO

Some pups take longer than others to react favourably to a lead. Although it is tempting to resort to a harness, which has the effect of lifting the pup bodily, rather than pulling from the neck, it is not recommended, because it will spoil the pet's future walking action.

(wicker would be chewed to pieces), his synthetic wool bedding and toys, the remainder of the base being covered with newspaper and housing a water bowl. The pup can sleep in the pen and be placed in it whenever you need to slip out for a few hours, thus alleviating any problem of chewed slippers – or furniture! The pen should be placed in a warm, draught-free position.

Also needed will be a feed bowl, soft puppy brush, and a puppy lead and collar. But please don't invest in a harness. It is admittedly easier to teach a pup to accept a lead with this item of equipment, but you risk spoiling its movement (*see* pages 38–9).

plastic bed

plastic bed

vet bed

padded bed

china bowl

metal bowl

plastic bowl

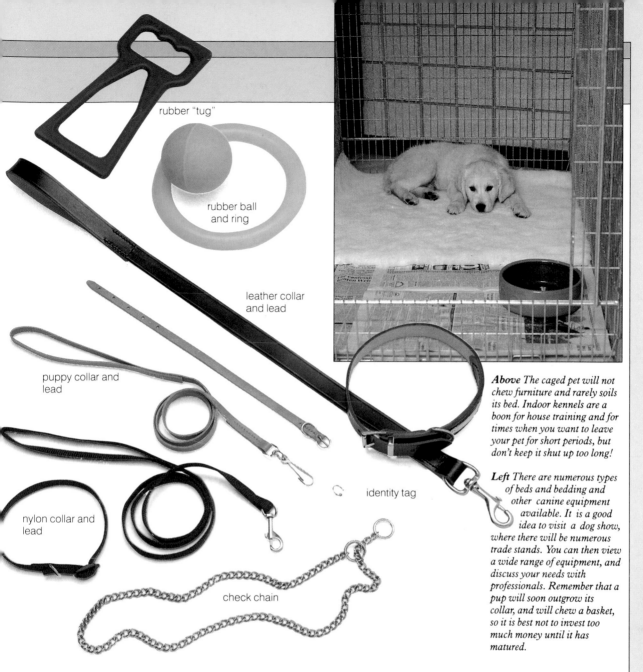

rubber "tug"

rubber ball
and ring

leather collar
and lead

puppy collar and
lead

nylon collar and
lead

identity tag

check chain

Above The caged pet will not chew furniture and rarely soils its bed. Indoor kennels are a boon for house training and for times when you want to leave your pet for short periods, but don't keep it shut up too long!

Left There are numerous types of beds and bedding and other canine equipment available. It is a good idea to visit a dog show, where there will be numerous trade stands. You can then view a wide range of equipment, and discuss your needs with professionals. Remember that a pup will soon outgrow its collar, and will chew a basket, so it is best not to invest too much money until it has matured.

KENNEL COMFORTS

Most pet dogs live in the house with their owners. Toy and short-coated breeds almost always do so. However owners of working and gundog breeds often prefer to kennel them out of doors. This does not involve less work. Kennelled dogs have to be fed, watered, groomed, exercised – and indeed cleaned out – just like their indoor counterparts. Heating should be provided in cold weather; heat lamps and space heaters are two of the systems widely used.

Check with the seller as to the pup's customary food – a breeder will give you a diet sheet. Even if you have other feeding plans, it is best not to alter the pup's dietary routine for the first few days.

Finally, do make sure that toys are of hard, durable plastic that cannot be swallowed; those of the old-fashioned rubber type are ideal. If your dog is destined to be a lightweight, think in terms of a carry box which will be a boon for transporting it to shows, the veterinary surgery, on holiday or simply for trips in the car. As a temporary measure, a cardboard carry box can usually be obtained from animal welfare societies.

GIVING YOUR DOG A PROPER DIET

BASICALLY, DOGS HAVE the same nutritional requirements as ourselves. They need a balanced diet containing protein (meat), carbohydrates (cereals) and fat with minerals and vitamins added. Almost all types of meat are suitable excepting liver, which is a laxative and should be fed only in strict moderation.

Water is essential and must be supplied either (almost always) as drinking water, or in the food itself. Minced meat contains about 70% water.

FRESH MEAT VERSUS BRANDED PET FOOD

It does not seem so long ago that conscientious dog owners insisted on feeding pets fresh meat, using prepared dog foods only as a standby. And indeed a diet of water, and suitable meat and biscuits do meet the basic food requirements of the dog in full.

Nowadays, however, branded pet foods have been scientifically prepared to meet the nutritional requirements of the dog and are fed by most kennels and individual dog owners, as much for the benefit of the dog as for convenience.

These prepared foods come in the form of meaty canned products, to which dog biscuits should be added, cans of complete or soft, moist foods which do not require the addition of biscuits, or a complete dry dog food to which only water is added. The dry foods do increase a dog's thirst, so if they are used, it is necessary to ensure that the drinking water supply is well topped up.

Above Dogs guard their food jealously. However, aggressive behaviour towards humans over the dinner bowl should not be tolerated.

And while many dog owners still insist on feeding pups on lightly cooked, lean minced beef for the first few weeks from weaning, canned puppy food is now available, which has been specially formulated to give pups a good start in life.

Puppy feeding schedule		
Age	Feeds per day	Approx time of feeds
From weaning to 3 months	4	Breakfast Lunch Tea Supper (optional bedtime drink, perhaps an egg switched in milk for large breeds)
3-6 months	3	Breakfast Tea Supper
6-12 months	2	Breakfast Tea (or early supper)
One year and over (The dog is an adult at one year)	1 or 2	Mid-day and/or early evening (If mid-day meal only is decided upon a few biscuits should be given at bedtime.)

Note The exact time of feeds is flexible, but once chosen must be strictly adhered to.

Initially the pup should receive two milky meals (a prepared baby food such as Farex is ideal) and two meals of lightly cooked, lean, minced beef or canned puppy food, with puppy biscuits.

Feeding the adult dog		
Quantities based on average 13 ½oz (380 g.) can		
Toy sized dog	e.g. Yorkshire terrier	¼-½ can
Small sized dog	e.g. West Highland White terrier	½ can
Medium sized dog	e.g. Cocker spaniel	1 can
Large sized dog	e.g. Labrador retriever	1 ½-2 cans
Very large sized dog	e.g. Great Dane	4 cans

It will be appreciated that some dogs burn up more energy, and have a greater need for food, than others, so once you have ascertained the correct weight for your dog you can adjust its rations accordingly. Consult your veterinarian if in doubt.

Dog food comes in a variety of forms. In the beginning you will need to try out different types of food to see which suits your dog best.

MEALTIME TIPS

- *If you feed a dog late at night you only have yourself to blame if it is not clean until morning.*
- *It does not matter whether you feed your adult dog once a day, or twice, dividing the food ration into two portions. However, toy breeds with small stomachs often fare better on two or even three little meals a day.*
- *On average a dog weighing 4.5kg (10lb) needs 225g (8oz) of food a day. A dog weighing about 11kg (25lb) needs 565g (1¼lb).*
- *Never ever give your dog poultry bones. They could be swallowed whole and splinter inside its stomach.*

semi-moist meat

tinned meat

complete dried food

fresh meat

dog biscuits

puppy mixer meal

chew sticks

vitamin treats

raw-hide chew

HOUSE-TRAINING

IT IS UNLIKELY that a pup will come to you ready house-trained, if for no other reason than that breeders, perhaps with several litters to look after, simply do not have the time.

Some pups are house-trained within a matter of weeks. Others take considerably longer. It is something that is achieved by diligence and patience, not by bullying or adopting the unpleasant habit of rubbing the pet's nose in the offending spot.

Most likely the pup has been conditioned to answering the call of nature on newspaper, and further paper training is recommended.

Once your pup has grown up it will be able to control its bladder for a matter of hours. In puppyhood it cannot do so, and you must be prepared for mistakes.

DO'S AND DON'TS

Spread newspaper fairly liberally on the kitchen floor and, whenever you see the pup about to squat, lift it up firmly but kindly, point to the paper and place it on it. Do this even if it has erred, but NEVER hit it if it has not used the newspaper.

Once the pup shows signs of understanding what is required, continue the practice, but substitute the generously spread paper with just a sheet or two at the back door. Once pup knows to toddle to the door when it wants to relieve itself you can start opening it and letting it out into the garden, praising it lavishly when it does what is required. But don't, please, leave it out in the cold for an inordinate length of time. Some dogs, like some people, take a little longer to understand what is required of them than others.

SOME BASIC RULES

- *If you are out at work all day, it is unfair to keep a dog no matter how much you may love them, unless, of course, you have a friend or helper who could be relied upon to call at your home every mid-day to exercise the pet in your absence.*
- *Never, ever hit a dog. Your tone of voice should be sufficient to express displeasure and a dog wants only to please. Be generous with praise whenever a dog does well, patting it , and saying "Good boy" or "Good girl" as the case may be.*

1 When your pup relieves itself, place it promptly on the sheets of newspaper that you will have placed on the kitchen floor.

2 Soon the pup will look for the newspaper when it needs to answer the call of nature and will toddle onto it but be prepared for the occasional mistake.

Obviously one does not want an adult dog to relieve itself in the house as a matter of course. However the mere fact of having been paper trained in puppyhood can be enormously beneficial in the case of tiny breeds if, for example, you are going out and know that your return may be delayed. In such a case, simply leave a sheet of newspaper by the door. The dog will know what it is there for.

HOW LONG TO LEAVE YOUR DOG?

New owners often ask how long they may leave their pet before returning to let it out into the garden. Bearing in mind that it is always best to leave a young dog only for short periods until it has had time to build up confidence in your return, it should, in adult life, be capable of being left for about five hours. There are, in most people's lives, the odd occasions which compel them to extend this period. However, the truth of the matter is that the person whose job demands their being out of the house from nine to five, should not consider dog ownership. The dirty, noisy and destructive dog is usually also a lonely one.

Below When you are fairly confident that the pup has performed, open the door, let the pup in, and praise it lavishly. It is always much easier to housetrain a pup when it has an older canine companion to show it the ropes.

3 Gradually decrease the amount of newspaper and leave a sheet or two by the back door.

4 Soon, if the weather is warm, you can open the back door when the pup heads towards it, and encourage it to go outside.

TRAINING YOUR DOG

YOUR PUP SHOULD NOT be taken for a walk until it has had its full quota of inoculations. This presents you with an ideal opportunity to prepare it for the adventure, by accustoming it to a lead and collar beforehand.

ATTACHING A COLLAR

First of all, let it get used to wearing a collar for short periods, making sure that it is not too tight. You should be able to place two fingers width underneath, without fear of it pulling over its head.

Now attach the lead and, after the pup has played with it for a little while, pick it up and place it at arm's length in front of you.

Next, holding the lead in your right hand, and offering a titbit with your left, pull the lead gently towards you. Once the pup gets the idea, start walking slowly backwards, gradually increasing the distance.

Once this exercise has been accomplished and the pup is no longer fighting the restriction of the lead and collar, you can begin leading it on your left hand side, reducing the number of titbits, but praising the pup's progress lavishly. But a word of warning: do not let this, or any other lesson, continue for too long, and always end on a note of encouragement.

GOING FOR "WALKIES"

Once the pup is bigger, and you venture out with it on to the road, it should walk on your left but, as I mentioned earlier, you should hold the loop of the lead in your right hand, but hold the part about half way up from the clip with your left, so that the lead extends across your body, and you are able to exert good control.

TEACHING "SIT" AND "STAY" COMMANDS

Regardless of whether you want your dog to be simply a household pet or to compete in obedience or conformation classes, it is necessary to teach it to "sit", to "stay" and to "come" when called. By teaching it the "stay" you could, for instance, prevent it from rushing across a road and having an accident or, indeed, causing one.

1

4

1 When lead training, have the dog walking on your left. Hold the end of the lead in your right hand, and take up most of the slack in your left hand. Give the command you are going to use, such as "heel", and walk off. Every time the dog pulls away, give a small jerk on the lead with your left hand, but release it again as soon as the dog returns to the correct position.

2 There are several ways in which to teach a dog to "sit". Here is one of the easiest: with the dog walking on your left, hold the lead up with your right hand and, with your left, firmly press the dog's hindquarters down, at the same time firmly

uttering the command "sit". Keep doing this during your walk until it gets the idea of what is required.

3 The "stay" is a progression from the "sit". Put your dog in the "sit" position. Now move in front of the dog, saying "sit", then "stay" very firmly, jerking on the lead if it attempts to move. If it does so, you must start again.

4 & 5 Tremendous patience is called for in dog training. Once the dog knows how to "sit" and "stay" you can begin using the command "stay" as you gradually move further away from it.

2

3

5

6

6 The "come" (or recall) is an advanced progression of the puppy lead training when you drew the bewildered pup towards you. Now you can adopt the same procedure uttering the command "come", once your pet is in the "sit-stay" position, and making a great fuss of it when it obeys, so that it associates the command with a pleasing experience.

REMEMBER...

- Dog training exercises should initially be taught with the dog's lead and collar on.
- A choke chain should not be used on a toy breed. These are frequently used in training large breeds, but increasingly they are being replaced with those of strong nylon, particularly where the practice of leading the dog from the head, rather than the neck, is adopted.
- Your dog's collar should be removed when it is at rest, and particularly before it goes to sleep at night. Not only is this more pleasant for the dog, but prevents the mark of the collar on its coat.

Above Training classes are an excellent place to teach your dog obedience, as you can work under the eye of a professional.

CAN I LEARN HOW TO SHOW MY DOG?

DON'T TRY TO RUN before you can walk is good advice. Yes, there are those who enter a Championship show with an untried dog and win their class, but this doesn't happen very often.

It is sensible to enrol your pup in a Ringcraft Class. In any case, you will not be permitted to exhibit it in Kennel Club recognized shows until it is six months of age.

The Ringcraft Class (not to be confused with the Dog Training Class, where your dog would learn obedience) is of help in accustoming the dog to mix with its own kind – and with people. You, in turn, will learn how to present your dog in the ring, using the correct technique for the breed.

For instance, while one would walk in the ring with a French Bulldog or a Toy breed, such as a Griffon Bruxellois or Chihuahua, it is necessary to run (gait) large breeds such as the elegant Afghan Hound or Doberman.

While Toy dogs are examined by the judge on a table, except for the perky Yorkshire Terrier, which is examined on its own show box, large breeds are examined on the ground, standing in show stance.

GETTING YOUR EYE IN

It is sound advice, before commencing your showing career, to attend as many dog shows as you can, and to watch handlers of your particular breed. Study how their dogs stand and move and try to emulate this in your practice sessions.

In the United Kingdom there are many Exemption Dog Shows, the word "Exemption" meaning that they are exempt from most Kennel Club rules. These shows are an excellent platform for the beginner and include fun classes, such as "the Dog with the Waggiest Tail", "the Dog in Best Condition" – and so on, and others for dogs that are not of pure breeding.

The Exemption is unlike the Sanction Show, which is open to members of the organising club only, while Open Shows and Championship Shows are for the seasoned exhibitor. It is at the latter that Challenge Certificates are on offer whereby one's dog or bitch may be chosen as the best example of its breed. Three Challenge Certificates awarded

Above Toy dogs are examined standing on a show table. Most aspirants practise standing their pet on the table for a few minutes each day from a very early age. This is something that can be done during the daily grooming session.

Left Ringcraft classes provide an excellent opportunity for a young dog to become accustomed to walking with its fellows and being examined by a stranger. The handler learns what to expect in the show ring and the various procedures involved. Classes are usually held on a weekday evening.

Above *A rosette such as this could be the reward for a Best in Breed win at a dog show.*

Right *A successful exhibitor demonstrates how to present a Hungarian Vizla in the show ring. Showing a dog is not as easy as it looks. It is important to select a breed in keeping with your own physical capabilities.*

DO'S AND DON'TS

Do *Always dress smartly in the show ring so as to complement your dog.*

Do *Wear sensible shoes if you are a lady exhibitor. Some shows are held in a muddy field – no place for perilously high heels.*

Do *Invest in a ring clip, so that the Judge and Steward can easily detect the number on your card.*

Do *Do study the catalogue carefully and make sure that you are at the ringside in time for your class.*

Do *Make sure that you take a bowl and water supply to the show for your dog.*

Don't *Chat with other exhibitors in the ring.*

Don't *Question the Judge's decision.*

Don't *Get cross with your dog if it does not perform as it might. "Every dog has its day!"*

by three different judges at three different Championship shows entitles the dog to be known as a Champion.

In America, Dog Matches are a good training ground for the novice. They produce awards, but not the necessary points towards championship status, which can only be achieved at Dog Shows.

Points towards a Championship are won at Specialist and All-Breed Shows, in five regular classes known as Novice, Bred by Exhibitor, American Bred, Open and Puppy (6–9 and 9–12 months). The winners of such classes subsequently have to compete against each other to select a Winning Dog. The same system then follows for Finals to select a Winning Bitch.

Judging systems vary from country to country but basically a winning dog in one country should be a winning dog in another. The judges are always looking for the dog which most exactly fits the standard for its breed.

GROOMING YOUR DOG

WHETHER PET OR SHOW DOG, your canine companion will benefit from a daily grooming. This daily beauty treatment not only makes your pet look and feel good, but gives the owner an opportunity to check for possible flea infestation or any minor injuries or other problems.

Of course some breeds need considerably more grooming than others, so if your time is strictly limited it is advisable not to choose a breed which requires intricate preparation, especially if it is destined for a show career.

Most short-coated breeds are fairly easy to look after. All they need is grooming with a brush of short, stiff bristles, or with a hound glove. A rub down with a velvet pad also works wonders and so does a brisk towelling. For heavy-coated breeds you need a brush with nylon bristles.

SHOW-TIME TURN-OUTS

● *Breeds that are fairly simple to prepare for the show ring: Boxer, Dachshund (smooth coat), Doberman, English Bull Terrier, French Bulldog, Smooth-coat Chihuahua and Griffon (Petit Brabançon), Pug, Staffordshire Bull Terrier.*
● *Breeds that require maximum preparation: Afghan Hound, Airedale Terrier, Wire-haired Fox Terrier, Bichon Frisé, Komondor, Lowchen, Llasa Apso, Poodle, Portuguese Water Dog, Pekingese, Old English Sheepdog, Puli, Shih Tzu, Yorkshire Terrier.*

CLIPPING, COMBING AND PLUCKING

There are some breeds, the show preparation of which is by no means easy for the novice to undertake. The Poodle, for example, needs its coat clipped about every six weeks and while the attractive lamb clip will suffice for a pet, an intricate lion cut is obligatory for show, and this can take many hours to perfect.

The glamorous Afghan Hound and popular Old English Sheepdog are but two breeds which require lengthy preparation, while terriers must be hand stripped; the Bichon Frisé clipped and elaborately scissored and the Hungarian Puli has the thick cords of its coat separated by hand. Other breeds, such as the comical little Griffon Bruxellois, must be knowledgeably plucked.

Usually the relevant breed club can supply information and a pattern chart of what is required.

Left It is sensible, when you buy a pup, to discuss with the breeder the basic equipment you will need. Later, if you decide to show the pup, you could require such items as portable trolleys for benching pens, grooming tables and show leads.

soft brush

rubber brush

hound glove

chamois sponge

wire comb

plastic comb

wire brush

ear wipes and eye wipes

nail clippers

toothbrush and paste

CROPPING AND DOCKING

Many working breeds (such as the Boxer, Great Dane and Doberman), Utility breeds (such as the Schnauzer) and Toys (such as the Miniature Pinscher and Griffon Bruxellois) have their ears cropped in their country of origin. However, the practice is illegal in the United Kingdom, Scandinavia, Australia and, depending on individual State law, in the USA. Tail docking has also been banned in Sweden, and controversy rages as to the rights and wrongs of this practice in other countries.

Canine beauty parlours will undertake the work for you, but most owners take pride in personally ensuring the immaculate turnout of their breed.

There are a number of routine jobs that must be done when you groom your dog. You must, for instance, remember to clean inside its ears with cotton wool moistened with olive oil, taking immense care not to probe too deeply; wipe away any stains around the eyes with cotton wool dipped in lukewarm water, or cold tea, and clean your dog's teeth with a proprietary brand of canine toothpaste.

It is not usually necessary to bath pet dogs except in summer-time when, after a brisk towelling, they can run about and get dry in the garden. However, show dogs are, in the main, bathed the night before, or a few days before a show, depending on the type of coat. This is a matter on which the breeder can best advise you.

Ears *Check the ears and ear flaps for any sign of wax or an unpleasant smell, which could be signs of canker. Ear wipes are available, but never probe the ear.*

Nails *If your dog gets plenty of roadwork, its nails should wear down naturally. If not, they will need to be trimmed with veterinary clippers about every 3 months. The veterinarian will undertake this task.*

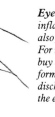

Eyes *Check the eyes for any inflammation and watering, also for opacity in the cornea. For routine care it is possible to buy eye wipes specially formulated to clean the discharge often found round the eye area.*

Teeth *It is sensible to take your dog to the veterinarian for regular descaling. This is particularly important in the case of Toy breeds, which can lose their teeth at an early age.*

CLIPPING AND CURLING

● *Some people buy a long-coated breed because they love grooming. They may sit, with their dog on their knees, all evening, meticulously working on its coat. If, unlike them, your time is limited, it is better to choose a short-coated breed.*

● *Dogs that receive regular pavement walks usually wear down their nails as a matter of course. Most breeds, however, need to have theirs clipped with veterinary clippers every few months. Take care not to clip beyond the quick (the white part of the nail) or bleeding and pain will be caused. Don't be afraid to ask the breeder, or your veterinary surgeon, to show you how to tackle this task.*

● *The perky little Yorkshire Terrier that you may see running around, covered in mud, is very different from its sedate, exhibition cousin, which spends most of its time wearing paper curlers.*

EXERCISING YOUR DOG

ALL DOGS NEED EXERCISE. There are breeds that can suffice with (indeed manage) very little exercise and others that need a great deal, so it would be unwise to buy a breed with limited walking capacity if you are an ardent rambler, or a large working breed if you are somewhat lethargic.

Most dogs need, on average, two good twenty-minute walks a day, preferably with some off-the-lead gambols in a suitable recreation area. If you have a fairly large garden, the latter is not so important, and you can play ball with your dog!

Working breeds, in particular, need plenty of exercise. If you can channel their energy and intelligence into a task such as obedience trials or agility, so much the better. You can start them off by enrolling at your nearest dog training club.

Toy dogs will keep happy and healthy with fairly limited exercise, but they enjoy a walk in the

OUT 'N' ABOUT

● *Lap dogs such as the Pekingese, Yorkshire Terrier and Pomeranian, enjoy nothing better than going for walks across the fields and getting gloriously muddy, but, when occasion demands, a walk in the park, or a romp in the garden, will suffice.*

● *Working breeds (e.g. the German Shepherd Dog, Doberman, Border Collie, Rottweiler and Mastiff) can become restless and ill-natured if they do not have a task to perform. These dogs were bred to serve man, not to spend their days in an apartment block.*

Below *A dog looks forward to its walk and will be disappointed if it does not occur at the usual hour. Often the owner would not themselves bother to exercise were it not for their canine companion.*

REGULAR ROUTINES

● *Do try and establish a regular timetable for your dog's walks; for instance, early morning and afternoon, and perhaps a short stroll at bedtime. Remember that once the routine is set, your dog will be disappointed if, at the appointed hour, its walk does not materialize, just as it would be if, at dinner time, its dish were not to appear.*

● *The dog whose master took it for an afternoon walk when it was a puppy will remember and wait eagerly to go out – sometimes long after its insensitive master has forsaken the habit.*

park and it would be wrong to deprive even a tiny Chihuahua of its daily outing. Some Toy breeds will literally walk their owners off their feet...

The Bulldog is a breed which cannot walk very far, certainly for no more than 1km (half a mile) – ideal for the retired, elderly gentleman! It is vital too that this breed is never taken out in very hot weather since, in common with other flat-nosed breeds which experience breathing difficulties, it might expire. Sensible owners never travel with these breeds during a warm spell without wet towels and ice packs with which to revive them.

TAKING PUPPIES FOR WALKS

It is unwise to take a pup, of any breed, for long walks until it reaches six months of age, by which time it should have the necessary physique and stamina. Obviously you could not expect even a large, adult dog, which was out of condition, and had previously led a sedentary life, to go on a 15-km (10 mile) walk. Distance must be worked up to gradually over a period of time.

The Dalmatian, originally a carriage dog, is a breed that will tirelessly follow a horse, but so will many a terrier breed. I once met a miniature dachshund walking over the hills, far from home, with its master. It seemed a wonder that the dog had got so far on its very short legs but, as its master explained, the dog had been taken for long walks all its life and could therefore manage the distance.

Left *A gundog such as this revels in country life and plenty of exercise.*

Above *The Dalmatian is traditionally a carriage dog. However, it is not a good idea to exercise your dog from a bicycle or a slowly driven car.*

SHOULD I PLAY WITH MY DOG?

IT IS NATURAL FOR DOGS to play, and even the games played as puppies can be the prelude to a useful working role. The pup that runs and fetches a ball is learning a first lesson in how to retrieve. A game of hide and seek can be a preliminary to tracking.

Puppies enjoy playing together and, in the act of play-fighting, learn about dominance and submission. They learn that it is possible to play-fight without having recourse to aggression – and that a bite can hurt! They chase and pounce, learning the rudiments of hunting, and they indulge in harmless sex play.

MOULDING YOUR DOG'S CHARACTER

A pup that becomes the companion of a withdrawn, introverted person, who does not play with it, is likely to develop into a serious dog with little sense of fun, unlike the pet of an outgoing individual which will be eager and friendly like its master. There is a saying that, "all work and no play makes Jack a dull boy". One could equally say that, "all sleep and no play make a dull dog".

Puppies are by nature lively, inquisitive and playful. But in fact the character of a dog is formed by the time it is ready to "leave the nest". The bold pup that comes forward to greet a visitor is destined to be an outgoing, fearless dog; the timid chap that slinks into a corner is likely to become a shy, nervous dog.

Above Dogs are wonderful companions for children. Playing ball is fun for both child and dog. For the latter it can be a first step in learning how to retrieve. The young handler should be encouraged to take her pet to a dog training class where it will learn to socialize with other humans and dogs.

ORDER OF THE COLLAR

- *Ever since ancient Egypt, paintings and sculptures have shown dogs wearing collars of various kinds. A wall painting in Pompeii shows a dog wearing a collar decorated with metal studs; a mosaic illustrates a chained dog wearing a plainer collar.*
- *The earliest collector of collars appears to have been Philip II of Spain who owned a collar that had belonged to the duke of Burgundy (1342–1404). It was described in the 1558 inventory of his possessions as being embroidered with pearls.*
- *Many collars from medieval times bore long, cruel-looking spikes, but these were intended to protect the dogs when they did battle with wolves and bears. Far more attractive to look upon is a large English brass collar from the late 18th century; it is inscribed:*

  I am Mr. Pratt's Dog, King St.
  Nr. Wokingham, Berks. Whose Dog are you?

WILL MY DOG SHOW AGGRESSION?

The dog communicates through a variety of body positions and facial expressions. The consecutive changes from normal stance to submission are shown here.

normal → arousal

play bow → play soliciting

submission → total submission

aggression → fearful aggression → fear

THERE ARE SOME BREEDS which were originally bred for their ferocity and guarding instincts, others that were purely designed as gundogs, pets, or for some other purpose. That is why it is so important to make the right choice for oneself.

Some breeds will accept other breeds into their social pack, and are gregarious with other dogs that they meet. Some are not. It is, however, unusual for a puppy not to be accepted though it should be introduced by easy stages, preferably on neutral ground.

It is a dog's instinct to guard its territory against all comers, hence the term watchdog, but while, for example, an Irish Setter would probably welcome a burglar with a lick and a wag of its tail, a Bull Terrier having let him in might then stand guard while the quaking wrongdoer stood on a chair.

COMPARING TEMPERAMENTS

Accepting then that a Cavalier King Charles Spaniel differs in temperament from a Rottweiler, and that there is no inherited flaw, a dog that has been carefully selected from sound stock, brought into the home at an early age, and properly trained, should not show aggression.

It is however essential, particularly in regard to the larger, guarding breeds, that they do not get their way too much when they are pups lest they should, in frustration, turn on their owner when they are disciplined at a later stage. Most dogs, let it be said, just want to please.

Above This picture of a contest between animals c. 5th century BC comes from a Greek painted-limestone relief at the National Museum in Athens. While man-and-dog fights were once common, the man sometimes having one arm tied behind his back, it is unusual to see two men with two dogs in a fighting pose.

Left Sometimes a court of law may order a dog to be destroyed or muzzled if it has a proven record of ferocity. In some countries an imported dog that has not been inoculated against rabies must be muzzled.

47

ANTI-SOCIAL BEHAVIOUR

IT IS IRONIC that while many people want a dog for its guarding abilities, which include the ability to bark, nobody wants a yappy, noisy one that is likely to evoke complaints from neighbours.

It is normal for dogs to give warning when there is a knock on the door, or a noise in the night. Some even give a bark of delight in play. However, the incessant barker cannot be tolerated and could even result in legal action being taken against its owner.

THE YODELLING DOG FROM THE CONGO

Some breeds are more noisy than others; Toy dogs, for example, are notoriously yappy – if they are allowed to get away with it – as are some small terriers, while the French Bulldog is a relatively silent fellow and, likewise, the Basenji, the barkless dog from the Congo, which gives only a kind of yodel.

TEACHING DOGS TO SPEAK

Just as it is possible to teach a dog to "speak" with a bark when it is shown a treat, then by lifting a warning finger encourage it to speak "softer, softer" until the mere whisper allows it the prize, so it is possible to prevent a dog from yapping persistently in everyday life.

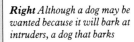

Right *Although a dog may be wanted because it will bark at intruders, a dog that barks persistently is a nuisance. Dogs must be taught at an early age to stop barking when ordered to.*

A rolled-up newspaper banged on the table will catch the dog off-guard, and should stop it barking. A vocal command should accompany your action: for instance, "NO".

Gently raising one's knee to a large dog's chest is a good way to prevent it from jumping up.

Water squirted over the dog from a hosepipe may be effective. This measure is sometimes adopted to stop dogfights.

DO'S AND DON'TS

Do *Kerb your dog. This means ensuring that it deposits excrement in the gutter, not on the footpath, and that you subsequently always remove it in a suitable receptacle.*

Do *Take out third party insurance lest your dog should cause a road accident or, perhaps, jump up at someone in play, tearing their clothing, or causing other damage.*

Do *Shut up your dog when visitors call, unless you are confident that they are dog lovers.*

Don't *Allow your dog to bark, taking it for granted that the neighbours don't mind. They probably do!*

Don't *Allow your dog to jump up at people. They may think that they are being attacked. Some people are very frightened of dogs!*

When the dog barks, walk into the room with a rolled up newspaper, bang it firmly on the table, and say "NO!" in your most disapproving tone, adding the words, "*Bad* boy" (or girl). The suddenness of the bang should stop the dog in its tracks and it will cease barking. A clap of the hands generally has the same result. Again, a disapproving tone is all important. Dogs do not like being in disgrace. Some will even slink off and sulk when they have been told off.

ANTI-SOCIAL BEHAVIOUR

As a dog owner you are under an obligation morally and, in some cases, legally, not to allow your pet to disturb or cause distress and inconvenience to others by, for instance, fouling public footpaths and verges or, worse, your neighbour's gate or garden frontage, and you must remove offending excrement should mistakes occur.

AN UNWELCOME WELCOME

Some people are passionately fond of dogs, others actively dislike them and could even interpret a boisterous, playful gesture on the part of the dog, such as rushing excitedly to the door with its owner, or leaping up at a visitor, as attack. In addition, no one wants a dog to jump up at them when it has muddy paws. Unless, therefore, you are confident that a visitor has a strong liking for dogs, or that your dog will not jump up unless invited to, it is always best to shut your dog in an indoor kennel, or at least in another room, out of sight, until the visitor departs. It is better to be safe rather than sorry.

Left *A poop scoop is the easiest way to clear up after your dog.*

Below *Members of the dog's family may enjoy an enthusiastic greeting, but it is unlikely to be appreciated by visitors. And a dog that jumps up when its paws are muddy is a nuisance to everyone. Puppies should be taught that this behaviour is not always appreciated.*

DOGS AND HOLIDAYS

OWNING A DOG does not mean an end to holidays, but it does mean making arrangements for your pet every time you decide to take a break, or even stay away overnight on a business trip.

Of course, you may have a reliable dog-loving neighbour who knows your dog and will be willing to take it in for the necessary period. Or its breeder may be more than willing to board it for you.

CHOOSING A GOOD BOARDING KENNEL

More likely, you will have to think in terms of booking your dog into a boarding kennel. Your veterinarian should be able to recommend establishments in your area. Pet shops and other dog owners can also generally supply helpful information and, likewise, public libraries, the

Left Some owners think it kinder to leave their dog with a friend but there is always the risk that it might slip out, which it is unlikely to do in a secure, well-run kennel.

Above Most exhibitors of toy breeds use travel cases or crates to transport them safely. Obviously the dog must be allowed out to relieve itself at regular intervals.

commercial section of telephone directories and your breed club.

Like popular hotels, good boarding kennels are booked up well in advance, so it is sensible to make your reservation as soon as you have made your own plans.

A reputable establishment will expect you to provide your dog's proof of inoculation against killer diseases such as canine distemper, leptospirosis, infectious hepatitis and parvo virus. Many now also require a certificate of inoculation against kennel cough. But don't be offended. You would not wish your pet to pick up a serious illness while in their care. Also required will be the name, address and telephone number of your veterinarian, your own contact number while away, and

CHECK IT OUT

● *Do make sure that your dog will have its own kennel, and that there are adequate heating arrangements, particularly if it is a short-coated breed.*

● *Do ask about exercising arrangements. It is preferable for each dog to have a separate exercise run, but in some cases a kennel maid will take a number of dogs for a walk together.*

● *There is usually a daily charge for dog boarding. Often this is based on the size of dog, i.e. toy, small, medium and large, but sometimes a standard charge is made irrespective of size.*

Left *Dogs must be kept under control when in a car. If you cannot fix a dog-guard in your car, use a dog harness, which can be obtained from most pet stores, instead.*

Below *There are many caravan and camping parks that welcome a well-behaved dog. It is sensible to check first, even if the chosen site does admit dogs, because they may have exceeded their quota.*

details of your pet's customary diet and of any special medication.

You should ask the proprietor to show you where your pet will sleep and enquire about exercise arrangements. Ideally dogs should have individual kennels and exercise runs, as well as some form of heating.

Ask about baskets, bedding and toys. Some kennels encourage owners to bring their pet's belongings, others would rather not take on this responsibility.

If it is your intention to board your dog for a number of weeks it might be sensible to book him in for a weekend beforehand, just so that he gets to know the routine, and realise that he has not been abandoned.

TRIPS AWAY

Of course many people do take their dogs on holiday with them (but not abroad, of course). There are hotels, particularly in country locations, that will accept pets. Motoring and hotel guides generally indicate whether this facility is available. In any case it is as well to check with the manager at the time of making one's booking rather than to turn up at the door with, possibly, a Great Dane.

Where dogs are accepted at hotels it is usual for them to be allowed to sleep in the owner's bedroom, but not to accompany them into public rooms or any place where food is being served.

Some caravan parks also welcome well-behaved dogs, particularly if they are kept on a lead.

INOCULATIONS AND HEALTH CARE

WITHIN LIVING MEMORY, the chances of rearing a healthy pup were slim because of the scourge of distemper. Nowadays, due to advances in veterinary science, the risks have been virtually eliminated. However, the prospect of a pup contracting Canine Distemper and several other killer diseases still exists and it would be sheer folly not to have your pup inoculated against them.

The age at which your veterinarian prefers to inoculate puppies may vary slightly. Generally, a first inoculation is given at about eight weeks, with a follow-up four weeks later. On no account should the pup be taken for pavements walks, or allowed to mix with other dogs, until the second inoculation has had time to take effect.

KEEPING INOCULATION RECORDS

It is customary, once a pup's inoculations have been carried out, for the veterinarian to provide the owner with a Record Card. Written thereon are the pup's name, breed, sex and age; also the type, and dose of vaccine given. A reminder may be sent in twelve months' time, inviting the owner to bring the pup into the surgery for a booster. In any case, as previously mentioned, proof of up-to-date inoculation will be necessary should you have occasion to book your dog into boarding kennels.

During the first few weeks after birth, pups are protected by antibodies received from their mother's milk – this is known as "maternally derived immunity". However, the protection wears off quickly and, thereafter, the pup may fall prey to all or any of the killer diseases, which is why vacci-

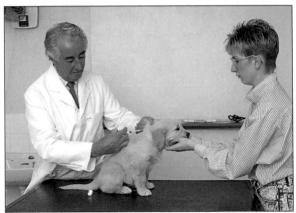

WORMING WARNING

Toxocara canis *is the common round worm deposited by infected dogs. If the resultant larva travels through the human body – for instance, where a child has touched dog faeces while playing in a sandpit, and subsequently puts fingers into the mouth – the result can be extremely dangerous. Hence the dire need for pups, and all dogs, to be wormed regularly.*

Above *Until a puppy's inoculations have had time to take effect, it is sensible for the owner to remove and disinfect their shoes when entering the home to minimize the risk of infection. You can exercise the puppy in a garden, or yard.*

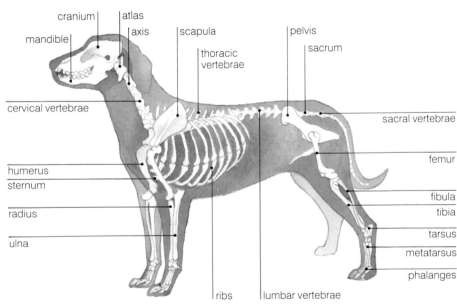

cranium
atlas
axis
mandible
scapula
pelvis
sacrum
thoracic vertebrae
cervical vertebrae
sacral vertebrae
femur
humerus
sternum
fibula
tibia
radius
tarsus
ulna
metatarsus
phalanges
ribs
lumbar vertebrae

nation is so important.

The inoculations which your veterinarian administers are likely to be those which provide protection against not only Canine Distemper, but also these:

● **Canine Parvo Virus** is a comparatively new disease first recorded in 1977. By the summer of 1978 it had become widespread with large-scale outbreaks as far apart as Canada and Australia. It was first recorded in the United Kingdom in 1979.

Parvo takes two forms – myocarditis or inflammation of the heart muscle in young pups up to eight weeks of age, and a severe gastro-enteritis or inflammation of the stomach and intestines from

1 When giving a pill, make sure that it is slipped right down the throat. Often a dog will secrete the pill in its mouth and spit it out afterwards.

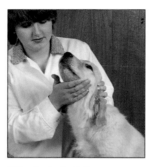

2 Stroke the dog's throat downwards to encourage it to swallow. Owners often disguise pills in a titbit, such as a piece of cheese.

FATAL FOR DOGS AND HUMANS

The killer disease Leptospirosis is caused by either of two micro-organisms. The disease is spread by bacteria shed in urine – lamp-posts are a serious source of infection. One form of Leptospirosis is generally contracted from rats and, under the name Weil's disease, can affect humans.

about five weeks through to adulthood. The death rate can be as high as 100% in young pups, but it reduces to around 10% in older pups and only about 1% in adult dogs.

Pups that survive myocarditis are frequently left with impaired heart function and may die prematurely, while survivors of the gastro-enteritis may remain in poor condition for a long period of time because of damage to the gut.

● **Canine Distemper** is caused by a virus that can attack virtually all of a dog's body tissues.

● **Viral Hepatitis** can cause damage to the liver, kidneys and eyes. It may also be responsible for respiratory infection.

● **Leptospirosis** damages the kidneys and liver.

You can see the extreme importance of not only having one's puppy inoculated but ensuring that booster inoculations are kept up-to-date.

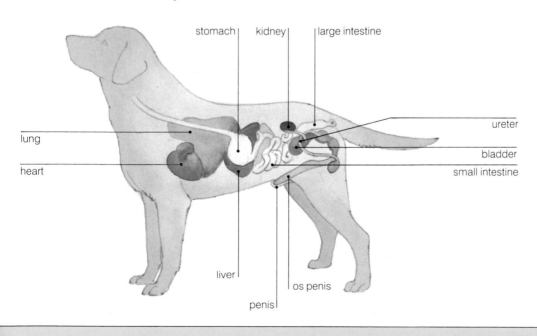

CANINE DISORDERS

AILMENT	SYMPTOM	ACTION
Anal glands	Dog will rub hindquarters on the ground, showing obvious signs of irritation.	Dogs have little scent glands on each side of the anus. If they become overfilled they cause irritation and, if not relieved, abscesses may develop. The task of emptying the anal glands can be undertaken by the dog's owner once the veterinarian has demonstrated the correct procedure.
Bad breath	see Worms (could be stomach disorder).	Tablets available.
Broken leg	–	Call the veterinarian without delay. Do not give anything by mouth. Move the dog as little as possible and try to immobilize the broken limb by, for instance, tying it to its partner on the opposite side of the body.
Canker	Continuous shaking of head and rubbing against floor and furniture.	Canker is the name usually applied to all types of canine ear infection stemming from an accumulation of wax due to dirt or mites. It is sometimes detected by an accompanying unpleasant smell. There are any number of preparations available but first ascertain the cause of the trouble by consulting your veterinarian. Warm olive oil acts as a cleansing agent. It could well clear up the trouble.
Choking	Dog may try to vomit or tear at mouth with paw.	Endeavour to open dog's mouth and remove foreign body – a piece of bone or a chew could have become wedged across the roof of its mouth. In some cases, a general anaesthetic may be needed, so check with your veterinarian.
Collapse	Dog will lie on its stomach and refuse to rise. May be breathing heavily.	Summon veterinary advice as soon as possible. Meanwhile, transfer patient onto a suitable mattress or blanket and keep warm. Bathe the mouth with glucose, or sugar in water. Do not force the dog to swallow. The dog should not be allowed to lie on one side for more than 20 minutes.
Cut foot	Sudden bleeding from foot, with or without lameness. This often occurs on beaches, and when dogs swim in ponds where there is broken glass. Similar symptoms may be shown when a claw is broken near its base.	If bleeding is profuse, wrap foot in lint or cotton wool and apply firm roller bandage with even pressure round the foot. Be careful not to bend a broken claw. Take the dog to a veterinarian for whatever treatment is necessary. Never use an elastic band or other constricting material.
Diabetes	Increased thirst and appetite, with associated weight loss.	Contact your veterinarian. You may have to learn how to give your dog daily injections of insulin.
Diarrhoea (acute)	Very loose motions that may contain blood; can be accompanied by vomiting and weakness in the hind legs.	Starve the dog and keep it warm. Bathe the mouth and gums with a warm solution of glucose or sugar in 1 pt of water. Phone the veterinary surgery for advice.
Earache	The dog will scratch its ear, or ears, and may hold its head on one side and shake it.	There may be a grass seed in the ear. Contact your veterinarian. Meanwhile, do not put anything in the ear. It is easy for owners to make the wrong diagnosis, so it is best to wait for professional treatment.
Eczema	Can be wet or dry. An angry patch appears on the dog's coat causing it to bite and scratch.	Causes range from diet deficiency to a hormone disorder. The veterinarian may try several treatments, from cream application to a course of injections, before the trouble is cleared up.
Fits	Sudden uncontrolled spasmodic movements, often with champing of the jaws; usually accompanied by salivation. The dog may fall onto its side. The muscles across the top of the head and down the neck may twitch violently.	Remove collar, if tight. Make sure that the dog cannot injure itself, for instance in a fireplace. Make sure that it can breathe by holding the head and neck, extended if necessary. Keep in a darkened, quiet room until you can get help, and prevent all sudden noises, door bells, slamming doors, etc. Most fits are over quite quickly. Seek veterinary advice as soon as possible.
Fleas	Scratching. Poor coat condition.	There are four common types of external parasite: lice, and their eggs (nits), which are found mainly in the dog's head; and fleas, ticks and mites, which may be found on its body. Treatment is available in the form of special shampoos, dusting powders and aerosols. Fleas are brownish and easily detectable in a dog's coat. They leave their droppings not their eggs, in the dog's coat.
Grass seeds	See Earache.	The seed may work its way into the ear canal, and should be removed by a veterinarian. Check that grass seeds – and items like chewing gum – do not become lodged in the paws.

AILMENT	SYMPTOM	ACTION
Heart attack	Usually self-evident. Often occurs in hot weather following exercise, particularly in the case of older – and flat-nosed – dogs.	Lay the dog on its right side with the head and neck extended. Open doors and windows to obtain as much fresh air as possible. If the tongue becomes blue, or breathing stops, massage the heart vigorously. Obtain veterinary help immediately.
Heat stroke	Panting and obvious distress.	Owners of flat-nosed breeds that are particularly susceptible to heat stroke should never travel without pre-soaked towelling dog coats and a supply of icy water. The latter should be applied to the dog's head. WARNING: Never ever leave a dog in a car without lots of ventilation.
Incontinence	The dog's inability to refrain from relieving itself for a normal period of time.	This is usually a sign of kidney failure as the dog approaches old age. The condition can be helped with medication.
Injured eye	One eye appears very sore, or is kept closed.	Look for, and carefully remove, any obvious foreign body, such as a grass seed. This may be done by washing the eye with clean, warm water and thus flushing out the foreign body. Keep the patient in semi-darkness. Take it to the veterinarian for treatment. If this is not possible immediately, put a drop of medicinal paraffin or olive oil in the eye as an emergency measure and prevent the dog from rubbing the affected eye with its paws, or on the furnishings.
Kennel cough	Persistent cough usually after a spell in boarding kennels.	Rarely serious. Prevention is better than cure as it is possible to vaccinate the dog by intranasal administration of a small dose of *Intrac*, using a specially designed applicator. Antibiotics should help existing sufferers.
Limp	–	This could be the result of something embedded in a paw, a cut, a torn muscle or ligament; or even in the case of an older animal, arthritis or rheumatism. Restrict the animal until the veterinarian has examined it.
Mange	Unsightly bare patches.	There are a number of varieties of mange: sarcoptic, demodectic, and otodectic, which affects the ears. It is caused by an infestation of mites, which burrow in the roots of a dog's coat. It is highly contagious and can be transferred not only from dog to dog, but also to humans. The necessity of washing one's hands thoroughly after applying ointment cannot be over-emphasized. The condition is curable, but it should be left to the veterinarian to recommend appropriate treatment.
Misalliance	Obvious: your bitch has accidentally been mated.	Your veterinarian can give an injection within 48 hours, but preferably within 24 hours, to prevent your bitch having puppies.
Poisoning	There may be sudden acute sickness, prostration or violent muscular movements.	There are many possible agents, including slug bait. If the dog is seen to swallow a known poison, induce vomiting by pushing a solution of salt (a teaspoonful in a tumbler of water for an average-sized dog) down the throat. Give milk if the substance swallowed is at all corrosive. *Never do this more than once.* Seek your veterinarian's advice quickly, taking with you the remainder of the poisonous agent, if known.
Road accident	You may witness the accident, or your dog may return injured or lame.	Restrain your dog if necessary to prevent further injury and get it and bystanders away from the road. Be careful with injured limbs. Put a cold compress using wet cotton wool or lint on any obvious bleeding points, but, above all, keep the dog warm and comfortable. Contact your veterinarian as quickly as possible. Don't leave your dog lying in the road.
Shock		Get the patient to a veterinarian as quickly as possible. Never give anything by mouth to an unconscious dog – it could choke and die.
Temperature		The best means of taking your dog's temperature is to insert the thermometer about 5 cm (2 in) into the rectum. The normal temperature is 38.9°C (101.5°F). A low temperature in dogs is serious – call the veterinarian.
Worms	Bad breath, poor coat, ravenous appetite, pot belly.	There are a numbert of types of worms: roundworms, tapeworms, hookworms, whipworms and, in some countries, heartworms. However, the most common is the roundworm (*Toxocara canis*), which is most prevalent in puppies and in bitches before and after whelping. At such times worming is often recommended by veterinarians at 2-weekly intervals. Normally, however, worming is recommended every 3 to 6 months. Many veterinarians will offer a wormer whenever a dog is presented for a booster inoculation.

SHOULD I HAVE MY DOG NEUTERED?

THE BITCH COMES INTO SEASON twice a year, the first season, or heat, occurring when she is about six months of age. It lasts on average for three weeks.

During the season, the bitch is attractive to male dogs. However, she is generally ready to be mated between the tenth to the twelfth day, after she has shown colour, although this can vary by a few days on either side. At this time the normally sedate bitch develops into a sex siren who will adopt every trick in the book to slip out and find a mate, irrespective of breed, while her owner may despair at

MILLIONS HOMELESS

It is estimated that as many as 10,000 cats and dogs are born every hour in the United States. The enormous scale of the problem is highlighted by the American Society for the Prevention of Cruelty to Animals (ASPCA): "Even if each family took in one of these animals, every American home would be filled within three years".

the sight of canine suitors hanging about outside the house.

Responsible owners keep a watchful eye on their bitch during her season, keeping her strictly segregated from male admirers, except in the case of a planned mating. Many people do keep an unneutered bitch, but it is as well to be aware of the extreme vigilance necessary.

SPAYING BITCHES

Neutering of the female, known as spaying, is the canine equivalent of a hysterectomy. The bitch which has been spayed no longer comes into season, cannot have puppies, and will not have false pregnancies. It is a logical step if you do not wish to breed from your bitch and if she is particularly difficult to cope with when she is in season.

Also, unless your bitch is of particularly good stock and there is likely to be a demand for her progeny, it is worth remembering the very many unwanted puppies which are, alas, destined to join the large band of strays.

Spaying, however, is not a decision to be taken lightly and the operation once carried out is irreversible.

Neutering (castration) of the male dog is not carried out so frequently, but is sometimes recommended by veterinarians, particularly in the case of aggression, over-ardent dogs, and those which share their home with bitches.

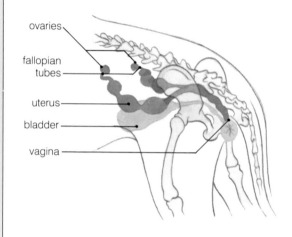

ovaries
fallopian tubes
uterus
bladder
vagina

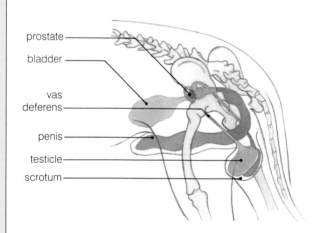

prostate
bladder
vas deferens
penis
testicle
scrotum

Above left *Spaying involves removing the reproductive organs of the bitch. An alternative method is to give the bitch a branded form of progesterone. This hormone prevents ovulation.*

Left *Castration – removal of the testicles of the male dog – is not performed frequently. Some owners think it is an easy remedy when an adolescent dog shows early signs of sexuality.*

WHAT IF I WANT TO BREED?

IF YOU HAVE DOG BREEDING in mind with the sole aim of making easy money, the immediate advice is "forget it!". Very few people make a living solely from dog breeding. Those who do are usually people who have had very many years experience of exhibiting behind them. Now they probably specialize in a number of varieties, and often run boarding kennels as well.

For the most part, dog breeders are hobbyists, keen exhibitors intent on producing the ideal specimen of their breed, and with little financial reward in view other than recouping from their breeding activities the expenses they have incurred in veterinary fees, entry fees for shows, and travelling expenses which are not inconsiderable when one realizes that Championship Shows may be held covering the length and breadth of one's country. There are few weekends in the show season when keen exhibitors are not on the road in the early hours of the morning when most people are tucked up in their beds.

If however you are determined to breed, it is advisable not only to have a few years showing experience first, but to invest thereafter in the very best bitch that you can afford. A "pet" quality bitch will produce only "pet" quality stock. You may say that you cannot afford the price, but it is far better to bide one's time and try to obtain a promising young bitch from a winning line, and subsequently mate her with a dog that has some form in the show ring. Possibly you may keep a bitch pup from her first or second litter, and gradually build up your breeding activities in that manner.

BREEDER'S TIPS

• *Toy breeds generally have small litters of about four pups compared with large breeds, such as the Irish Setter and Golden Retriever, which can have seven pups or more. There are no hard and fast rules and it is believed by some that the day of mating can determine the number of pups in a litter.*

• *The novice breeder would be advised to steer clear of breeds with large heads (such as French Bulldogs, Pekingese, Boston Terriers) which are more prone than others to require caesarian delivery.*

• *Golden Retrievers, West Highland White Terriers, and Cavalier King Charles Spaniels are three breeds often chosen by the aspiring dog breeder.*

Right *This family of Rhodesian Ridgebacks show the finest qualities of many European breeds blended with those of the Hottentot Hunting Dog. Note the distinctive ridge running from behind the shoulders to the haunches.*

1 It is normal to take the bitch, when it is ready for mating, to the stud dog. If time permits, it is helpful if the pair have a chance to run together and become acquainted before the mating takes place.

2 Dogs will usually mate without human assistance, but not always. When assisting the mating of large breeds, a handler supports the bitch with his knee and also guides the dog, the bitch being firmly held by its owner. With toy breeds, a larger brood bitch is preferred. The dog is positioned on a block to give it the required height.

3 After a mating the dogs will tie. They will eventually break away naturally. The tie is not always necessary for a successful mating.

THE BITCH IN WHELP

IT IS NOT EASY in the first few weeks following mating to determine whether your bitch is in whelp. Even a veterinarian would be unlikely to feel the tiny foetuses under four weeks.

However, about the fifth week, previous to which the bitch may have carried the litter high in the rib cage, you will notice certain changes: her teats will start to develop and grow pink in colour, she may seem greedy for food and appear generally more maternal and loving.

At this stage, the bitch requires a third more food than usual. It should be mainly protein. Don't feed her up with starchy foods or these will result in her putting on too much weight.

Daily exercise should not be neglected until this

causes discomfort. It is good for the bitch to keep her muscles active – also to be gently exercised following the birth to help regain her figure.

When the bitch reaches the seventh week of pregnancy the litter will be carried downwards, protruding low in the body. Now there may be less appetite because of the reduction of space in the abdomen. You can help by providing feed in the form of three or four small meals rather than one large one. Be prepared to bear with the bitch if she neglects her normally fastidious toilet habits. This also is because of pressure in the abdomen. She will be clean again after the birth.

THE WHELPING BOX

Remember that the pups will be coming into the world from a much warmer environment. Therefore, the whelping box, lined with newspaper, should be positioned where there is constant heat. It is important, particularly in the case of Toy breeds, that the temperature at time of birth is about 27°C (80°F) and that this does not fall below 21°C (70°F) for the first three weeks of the puppies' life.

Left *The Great Dane is a breed that needs warmth and, despite its size, it is often whelped in a cosy corner of the kitchen. If you are considering keeping this variety, remember that it is expensive to feed.*

CHECKLIST

What will you need for the maternity ward?

- *washable bedding, preferably of the synthetic sheepskin type*
- *newspapers*
- *roll of paper tissues*
- *scissors*
- *cotton wool*
- *baby feeder – you may have to hand feed the puppies*
- *towel*
- *clock, to time the intervals between births*
- *pen*
- *paper*
- *your veterinarian's telephone number*

NOTE: The average time between births of the first pup and the second range from 20–40 minutes, averaging 30 minutes between births. If the pups have not all appeared within three hours of the start of labour, or if the bitch is in distress, call your veterinarian immediately. You should have alerted him that the litter was due!

WEANING AND HOME-FINDING

THE BITCH WILL FEED HER PUPS, and clean up after them, for the first four weeks. However, at that time – sometimes before if she is not a very maternal bitch – she will want to revert to her normal way of life. She has done her job and now yours begins.

You can commence weaning by shutting the bitch away from the pups for a few hours a day until she is finally spending only the night with her litter.

The pups should be totally independent by the time they are six weeks of age, but this is rather young for them to go to new homes. Eight or preferably ten weeks is recommended.

Nowadays, with prepared puppy foods on the market, weaning puppies is considerably easier. However, any milky baby food, with glucose added, is an excellent starter to get pups lapping. Dip a finger in the saucer and allow them to lick. They will soon get the idea.

There are preparations formulated from skimmed milk to equate as near as possible with bitch's milk and this is also recommended. It is also beneficial for the bitch herself prior to whelping.

Once the pups are taking their milk meals, you can introduce lean minced beef, raw, or preferably lightly cooked. Be sure that they are well weaned on to their two milk meals and two meat meals a day before they go to new owners.

It is not as easy as you might think to find good homes for puppies. You can, of course, put an advertisement in your local newspapers and post cards in shop windows. Much better, however, is to try and obtain bookings through the breed club or canine newspapers as soon as your bitch is in whelp, and to let your veterinarian know of the impending arrival. He may know someone who is looking for a pup – perhaps someone who has just lost an old canine companion.

Don't forget to give buyers a feeding chart along with the pedigree and transfer documents, and perhaps a little note asking the buyer to return the puppy to you if it does not suit. Better surely to have it returned to your care for rehoming than for it to end up, for some reason, in a pound. You should also let the buyer know the dates on which your puppies were wormed and hand over the vaccination record card if you have had the first inoculation(s) administered.

Sometimes breeders take out an insurance against veterinary fees for the first few months of the pup's life; full details should be given to the buyer in case of a claim or if they should wish to renew the insurance cover when it expires.

Left *Irish Setters often have large litters. Before the puppies go to their new owners, the breeder must make sure the pups can take milk and meat feeds.*

Above *The strongest pup will always try to take the lion's share. It is important to make sure that all the pups get their fill.*

WORMING WARNING

Pups should be wormed at five weeks and, again, at seven weeks. Adults should be wormed at six-monthly intervals.

How Long Will My Dog Live?

DOGS, LIKE PEOPLE, ARE, alas, subject to illness and accident. Just as one member of a human family may outlive their brothers and sisters, so a litter member may have a longer, or shorter, lifespan than its fellows.

On average, a dog's lifespan is about twelve years. With advances in veterinary skills many are living several years longer. There are, however, breeds which are known for their longevity or otherwise.

The Great Dane, for instance, rarely goes beyond seven to nine years, likewise, the Bulldog. Poodles, Yorkshire Terriers, Chihuahuas, Schipperkes and small terriers, on the other hand, often live well into their 'teens.

You will also find that very often the dog whose parents and grandparents have lived to a great age is likely to do so too.

An Eye For An Eye

The longest serving guide dog in Britain is reckoned to have been Emma, a black Labrador Retriever which belonged to Sheila Hocken of Stapleford, Nottinghamshire, who later wrote a best-selling book (Emma and I) about her seeing-eye dog. Emma had performed her duties for eleven years when, remarkably, Sheila (who had been born blind) had her sight restored after an operation. Not long after, Emma herself developed cataracts and when her sight failed they swapped roles, Sheila Hocken guiding her faithful dog around. Emma died at the ripe old age of 17 in November 1981, having the added distinction of being the oldest Guide Dog for the Blind on record.

Left *The Bulldog is a delightful companion. Sadly, however, it rarely lives beyond 8 or 9 years. Its walking capacity is about ½ mile. It should never be exercised in hot weather.*

Below *The perky Yorkshire Terrier may live well into its teens. This show dog is far removed from the pet Yorkies that revel in getting gloriously muddy.*

Keeping Snug and Well

● *Old dogs, in common with old people, feel the cold. Make sure that they have adequate heating.*
● *Toy breeds, and all those with short coats, benefit from the protection of a coat when being exercised in winter.*

CARE OF THE ELDERLY DOG

AGAIN, IN COMMON WITH HUMANS, the dog's organs wear out with age – it suffers from heart, kidney and liver failure.

Because of veterinary skills there is no reason to fear that because an elderly dog begins to ail, death is imminent. What is important is that any weakness is detected in time for treatment to be effective.

The dog's hearing and eyesight may, for example, begin to deteriorate slowly from the age of about eight, and it is from this time onwards that regular examinations by your veterinarian are more than ever necessary.

For instance, a little cough that you had disregarded could be the onset of a heart condition which, if caught in time, should enable your pet, with medication to live out its lifespan.

Because your dog is getting old there is no need to change its routine drastically. If, for example, you have taken a walk together at certain times every day, continue to do so, but cut down on the duration of the walks. Similarly, you may find that your dog copes better with two smaller meals than with one large meal a day.

I always think that having an elderly dog to look after is rather like caring for a puppy again. A dog always needs its owner, but the dependence of puppyhood becomes pronounced again in old age.

Above *Dogs are a great comfort to the elderly. Often they are the remaining link with a lost partner. Regular veterinary check-ups from the age of 8 should enable the veterinarian to spot any defect and take action to prolong the ageing pet's life.*

GROWING OLD TOGETHER

- *Should an elderly person keep a dog? What if they should predecease their pet? This is a question that often crops up, particularly in the case of lonely old people who live alone, and would love to have a canine companion.*
- *Obviously it is ill advised for a frail, elderly person to keep a large, powerful dog. But there is no reason why they should not keep a pet as long as arrangements are made in advance for the animal's welfare in the event of its owner's death.*
- *Have a chat with the breeder at the time of purchase. Perhaps they will agree to take the dog back. Certainly they will be able to give you the address of the breed rescue society. There are also various animal charities which will undertake to look after a pet for the rest of its natural life in return for a bequest, or life-time subscription.*

DOG BREEDS

BREEDS OF THE WORLD INTRODUCTION

FROM THE TIME THAT dogs first became domesticated, they have been selectively bred by humans for different purposes, such as hunting, herding or guarding. In more recent times they have gradually been bred for more and more specialized tasks, leading to the great diversity of dog breeds recognized today.

In the following breed descriptions, information is provided on the origins and development of each breed, together with its characteristics and temperament, acceptable size range and colour varieties.

AFGHANISTAN
- Afghan hound

AUSTRALIA
- Australian cattle dog
- Australian silky
- Australian terrier
- Kelpie

AUSTRIA
- Austrian coarse haired hound
- Austrian hound
- Austrian shorthaired pinscher
- Tyrolean hound

BELGIUM
- Belgian sheepdogs (Groenendael – Malinois, Tervueren – Laekenois)
- Bouvier des Ardennes
- Bouvier des Flandres (Belgium – France)
- Griffon Brabancon
- Griffon Bruxellois
- Schipperke
- St Hubert Bloodhound

BRAZIL
- Brazilian Guard dog
- Brazilian tracker

CANADA
- Eskimo dog
- Landseer
- Newfoundland

CHINA
- Chow Chow
- Pekingese
- Shar-Pei

CUBA
- Havana Bichon

CZECHOSLOVAKIA
- Black Forest hound
- Czech (Cesky) terrier
- Czech coarse haired setter (Cesky)
- Slovakian Chuvach (Kuvak)

DENMARK
- Gammel Dansk Honsehund

EGYPT/ARABIA
- Pharaoh hound
- Saluki
- Slughi

FINLAND
- Finnish hound
- Finnish spitz
- Karelian bear dog
- Lapponian herder

FRANCE
- Anglo French white and black
- Anglo French white and orange
- Anglo French Tricolor
- Ariege setter
- Ariegeois
- Artois hound
- Basset Griffon Vendeen
- Beauce shepherd
- Bichon frise
- Billy
- Blue Auvergne setter
- Blue Gascony Basset
- Bordeaux Mastiff (Dogue de Bordeaux)
- Bourbonnais setter
- Briard
- Brittany spaniel
- Coarse haired Griffon
- Dupuy setter
- French Setter
- French spaniel
- French Tricolor
- French white and black
- French white and orange
- Grand Griffon Vendeen
- Great Anglo French Tricolor
- Great Anglo French white and black
- Great Anglo French white and orange
- Great Gascon of Saintonge
- Great Gascony blue
- Levesque
- Lowchen
- Nivernais Griffon
- Norman Artesian Basset
- Papillon
- Phalene
- Picardy shepherd
- Picardy spaniel
- Poitevin
- Pont-Audemar spaniel
- Poodle (Germany often credited)
- Porcelaine
- Pyrenean mountain dog (Great Pyreneed)
- Pyrenean smooth faced shepherd
- Pyrenees shepherd
- Small Anglo French
- Small blue Gascony Griffon
- Small Gascon of Saintonge
- Small Gascony blue
- Small sized French setter
- St Germain setter
- Tawny Brittany Basset
- Tawny Brittany Griffon
- Vendeen Griffon Briquet
- Woolly haired Griffon

GERMANY
- Affenpinscher
- Bavarian mountain hound
- Boxer
- Dachsbracke
- Dachshund
- Doberman
- German hunt terrier
- German pointer (Short, Long-haired, rough)
- German shepherd dog
- German spaniel
- German Spitz
- Great Black Spitz
- Great Dane
- Great Spitz
- Hanover hound
- Hovawart
- Kromfohrlander
- Leonberger
- Munsterlander
- Pinscher
- Pomeranian
- Pudelpointer
- Rottweiler
- Schnauzer (Giant, Standard, Miniature)
- Steinbracke
- Weimaraner
- Wesphalian Basset

GREENLAND ARCTIC – FAR NORTH
- Greenland dog
- Samoyed

HOLLAND
- Drentse Patrijshond (partridge dog)
- Dutch setter – short – long-haired
- Dutch shepherd (coarse – smooth-haired)
- Keeshond
- Stabyhoun
- Wetterhoun (Dutch spaniel)

HUNGARY
- Hungarian coarse-haired setter
- Hungarian Greyhound
- Hungarian Vizla
- Komondor
- Kuvasz
- Mudi
- Puli
- Pumi
- Transylvanian hound

ISRAEL
- Canaan dog

ITALY
- Bergamese shepherd
- Bolognese
- Cirneco dell'Etna
- Italian coarse haired Segugio
- Italian Greyhound
- Italian setter
- Italian shorthaired Segugio
- Italian Spinone
- Italian spitz
- Maltese terrier (controversy: Malta or Italy)
- Maremma sheepdog
- Neopolitan mastiff

JAPAN
- Ainu dog
- Hokkaido dog
- Japanese Akita (Akita Inu)
- Japanese Chin (Spaniel)
- Japanese fighting dog
- Japanese spitz
- San Shu dog
- Shiba Inu

MEXICO
- Chihuahua
- Chinese Crested Dog (via China)
- Mexican Hairless (Xoloitzcuintli)

MOROCCO
- Atlas dog

NORWAY
- Norwegian sheepdog (Buhund)

- Otterhound
- Pointer
- Red and white setter
- Rough collie
- Scottish terrier (formerly Aberdeen terrier)
- Sealyham terrier
- Shetland sheepdog
- Skye terrier
- Smooth collie
- Soft coated wheaten terrier
- Staffordshire bull terrier
- Sussex spaniel
- Welsh Corgi Cardigan
- Welsh Corgi Pembroke
- Welsh springer spaniel
- Welsh terrier
- West Highland white terrier
- Whippet
- Yorkshire terrier

- Bernese mountain dog (cattle)
- Entlebucher cattle dog
- Great Swiss cattle dog
- Jura hound
- Lucerne hound
- Small Bernese hound
- Small Jura hound
- Small Lucerne hound
- Small Swiss hound
- St Bernard
- St Hubert type jura hound
- Swiss coarse haired hound
- Swiss hound

- Norwegian Elkhound (Gray)
- Norwegian Elkhound (Black)
- Dunker
- Haldenstover
- Hygenhund
- Lundehund

POLAND

- Polish hound
- Tatra shepherd
- Valee shepherd

PORTUGAL

- Castro Laboriere dog
- Estrela mountain dog
- Portuguese mountain dog
- Portuguese Podengo (Giant, Medium, Dwarf)
- Portuguese setter
- Portuguese water dog
- Rafeiro do Alentejo

RUSSIA

- Borzoi

SOUTH AFRICA

- Basenji
- Rhodesian Ridgeback

SPAIN

- Burgos setter
- Catalonian shepherd
- Ibizan hound – smooth, coarse, longhaired
- Pyrenean mastiff
- Spanish greyhound
- Spanish hound
- Spanish mastiff

SWEDEN

- Drever
- Hamiltonstovare – Hamilton hound
- Jamthund
- Lapland spitz
- Norrbottenspets
- Schillerstovare (hound)
- Smalandsstovare
- Swedish Gray Dog
- Vastgotaspets

SWITZERLAND

- Appenzeler cattle dog
- Bernese hound

TIBET

- Lhasa Apso
- Shih Tsu
- Tibetan Mastiff
- Tibetan spaniel
- Tibetan terrier

UNITED KINGDOM AND IRELAND

- Airedale terrier
- Beagle
- Bearded collie
- Bedlington terrier
- Border collie
- Border terrier
- Bull terrier
- Bulldog
- Cairn terrier
- Cavalier King Charles spaniel
- Clumber spaniel
- Curly coated retriever
- Dandie Dinmont terrier
- Deerhound (Scottish)
- English Cocker spaniel
- English setter
- English springer spaniel
- English toy terrier
- Field spaniel
- Flat-coated retriever
- Fox terrier smooth
- Fox terrier wire-haired
- Foxhound (English)
- French bulldog (French also claim credit)
- Golden retriever
- Gordon setter
- Greyhound
- Harrier
- Irish setter
- Irish terrier
- Irish water spaniel
- Irish wolfhound
- Jack Russell terrier
- Kerry blue terrier
- King Charles spaniel
- Labrador retriever
- Lakeland terrier
- Lancashire heeler
- Manchester terrier
- Mastiff
- Miniature bull terrier
- Norfolk terrier
- Norwich terrier
- Old English Sheepdog (Bobtail)

UNITED STATES OF AMERICA

- Alaskan Malamute
- American Foxhound
- American Staffordshire terrier (Pit Bull/Yankee terrier)
- Basset hound
- Black and Tan Coonhound
- Boston terrier
- Chesapeake Bay retriever
- Siberian husky

YUGOSLAVIA

- Balkan hound
- Bosnian coarse haired hound
- Charplaninatz
- Croatian shepherd
- Dalmatian
- Istrian coarse haired hound
- Istrian short haired hound
- Karst shepherd
- Posavatz hound
- Yugoslavian mountain hound
- Yugoslavian tricolor hound

65

THE DOG CLASSIFICATIONS: GROUPS

DOGS ARE DIVIDED into distinct groups according to the purpose for which they have been bred. This aids classification at shows and enables visitors to know the day and section when and where their favourite breeds can be found. Reading about the groups also enables the buyer to decide which group includes varieties most suitable for their lifestyle – the sportsman, for instance, perhaps scorning the Toy Group, which might hold tremendous appeal for his wife.

UTILITY GROUP

There is an exception to the obvious naming of groups: the one that is described as "Utility". This is reserved for dogs which are not Toys, and have not been bred for any specific purpose. Many of the traditional pet breeds are to be found in this classi-

fication, and so are new breeds and those which may have been newly imported from their country of origin for which no ready classification can be found.

Many popular pet dogs fall within the Utility category, including the Dalmatian, Chow Chow and Shar Pei, the Schipperke and the charming Japanese Spitz. But bear it in mind that, because a breed is in the Utility Group today, it may not necessarily be there tomorrow!

If you are planning to attend a big dog show – one, for example, that is run over a number of days – it is particularly important to familiarize yourself with the Groups. Utility and Toy may, for instance, be exhibited on one day, and Hounds and Working breeds on another.

Left The Schipperke comes from Belgium, where it was used by sailors to guard their boats. It makes a good house dog and family pet.

Above For many centuries the Laso Apso existed only in Tibet, where it was used to guard monasteries. It arrived in the West in the 20th century.

UTILITY
Boston Terrier
Bulldog
Canaan Dog
Chow Chow
Dalmatian
French Bulldog
German Spitz (Klein)
German Spitz (Mittel)
Japanese Akita
Japanese Spitz
Keeshond
Leonberger
Lhaso Apso
Miniature Schnauzer
Poodle (Miniature)
Poodle (Standard)
Poodle (Toy)
Schipperke

Schnauzer
Shar-Pei
Shih Tzu
Tibetan Spaniel
Tibetan Terrier

WORKING GROUP
Alaskan Malamute
Anatolian Shepherd Dogs
Australian Cattle Dogs
Bearded Collie
Belgian Shepherd Dog (Groenendael)
Belgian Shepherd Dog (Laekenois)
Belgian Shepherd Dog (Malinois)
Belgian Shepherd Dog (Tervueren)

Left The mastiff is loyal and suspicious of strangers, and is used as a guard dog.

Below The Border Collie is among the most popular of working breeds. It originates from Scotland, but is now used all over the world for working with sheep.

Bernese Mountain Dog
Border Collie
Bouvier Des Flandres
Boxer
Briard
Bullmastiff
Collie (Rough)
Collie (Smooth)
Dobermann
Eskimo Dog
Estrela Mountain Dog
German Shepherd Dog
(Alsatian)
Giant Schnauzer
Great Dane
Hovawart
Hungarian Puli
Komondor
Lancashire Heeler

Maremma Sheepdog
Mastiff
Neapolitan Mastiff
Newfoundland
Norwegian Buhund
Old English Sheepdog
Pinscher
Portuguese Water Dog
Pyrenean Mountain Dog
Rottweiler
St Bernard
Samoyed
Shetland Sheepdog
Siberian Husky
Swedish Vallhund
Tibetan Mastiff
Welsh Corgi (Cardigan)
Welsh Corgi (Pembroke)

THE WORKING GROUP

The working group is the one in which you find breeds originally bred as guards and protectors of sheep and other livestock. Within this Group, as might be expected, are found the Doberman, German Shepherd and Rottweiler, sheepdogs such as the Border Collie and Old English Sheepdog, and many other breeds designed to perform a guarding and protecting role in their native land.

Some of these breeds, originally bred for ferocity, have through careful breeding now emerged as gentle pets. However, it must be remembered that instincts prevail, and that the majority of dogs in this group are happiest and healthiest when they have access to open spaces and a job to do.

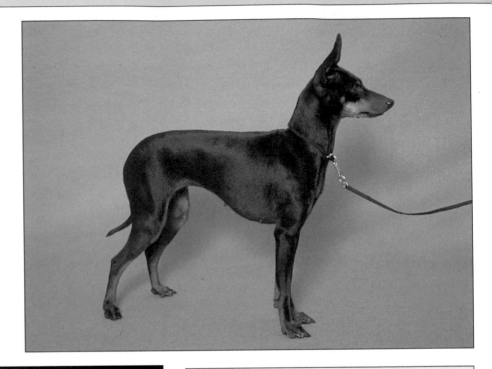

Right The English Toy Terrier is the toy version of the Manchester Terrier, and is not often seen these days.

Below The Bichon Frise is descended from the Maltese Terrier, and was popular in the courts of Europe during the 16th and 17th centuries. It subsequently became a successful circus performer.

TOY GROUP

The Toy group comprises those breeds which have been bred solely as diminutive companions, and the traditional lap dogs are to be found in this category. The newcomer will, however, find some surprises. The Toy Poodle, for instance, is not in this Group, but is to be found alongside the Miniature and Standard Poodle in the Utility Group, while the perky Yorkshire Terrier has a place in the Toy

TOY GROUP
Affenpinscher
Australian Silky Terrier
Bichon Frise
Cavalier King Charles
Spaniel
Chihuahua (Long Coat)
Chihuahua (Smooth Coat)
Chinese Crested Dogs
English Toy Terrier (Black &
Tan)
Griffon Bruxellois
Italian Greyhound
Japanese Chin
King Charles Spaniel
Lowchen (Little Lion Dog)
Maltese
Miniature Pinscher
Papillon
Pekingese
Pomeranian
Pug
Yorkshire Terrier

Group and not with his larger terrier relations.

The smallest Toy breed is the Chihuahua, the standard weight for which is up to 2.7kg (6lb) with 1–1.8kg (2–4lb) preferred, followed by the Yorkshire Terrier whose weight should be no more than 3.1kg (7lb). However, it will be appreciated that these and other weights – and indeed heights – mentioned are those desired for exhibition purposes, and there are many happy, healthy examples of their breeds which are bigger, smaller, heavier or lighter than their standard dictates.

The largest member of the Toy Group is the Cavalier King Charles Spaniel, the requirement for which is a well-balanced dog within 5.5–8kg (12–18lb).

Don't be misled into thinking that Toy dogs are purely ornamental. They enjoy being exercised and make excellent small guards.

THE TERRIER GROUP

The terrier group is self-explanatory: it comprises those lively dogs which were predominantly bred to hunt small animals, like rats and foxes. They are affectionate and make good pets, but they are extremely lively, bouncy dogs, not averse to the occasional scrap. The terrier would make a first-class companion for the young, but it is not ideally suitable for a sedate, elderly lady, although they can be immensely loving.

Terriers come in various sizes, one of the most popular being the West Highland White Terrier, (or "Westie"), a white terrier which stands approximately 28cm (11in) at the withers. The Airedale

Terrier is the biggest terrier, 58–61cm (23–24in), bitches slightly less, as is usually the case.

The Bull Terrier and the Staffordshire Bull Terrier are the least terrier-like in appearance of this Group's members, but it must be borne in mind that the Bull Terrier has an extinct white terrier in

Below *The Bedlington was first bred in the 18th and 19th centuries for catching vermin and other small animals. It was particularly popular with poachers.*

Bottom *The Skye Terrier is an old breed that has contributed to the development of many of the Scottish terrier breeds.*

TERRIER GROUP
Airedale Terrier
Australian Terrier
Bedlington Terrier
Border Terrier
Bull Terrier
Bull Terrier (Miniature)
Cairn Terrier
Dandie Dinmont Terrier
Fox Terrier (Smooth)
Fox Terrier (Wire)
Glen of Imaal Terrier
Irish Terrier
Kerry Blue Terrier
Norfolk Terrier
Norwich Terrier
Parson Jack Russell Terrier
Scottish Terrier

Sealyham Terrier
Skye Terrier
Soft-Coated Wheaten Terrier
Staffordshire Bull Terrier
Welsh Terrier
West Highland White Terrier

its make-up, while the "Staffy" descends from Bulldog-terrier stock.

It is a common mistake to mix up the West Highland White Terrier with the Scottish Terrier, the latter being, in fact, an all-black dog, once known as the Aberdeen Terrier.

THE GUNDOG GROUP

Gundogs, designed to retrieve gamebirds and water fowl, are, in the main, gentle, companionable animals which combine admirably the role of sportsman's dog and household pet – such as the Golden Retriever and Labrador Retriever.

Again there is a great variety of Gundogs to choose from, ranging from the Cocker Spaniel (the "Merry Cocker") to the bigger setters, retrievers and pointers.

The setter is bred to "sett", to stand rigid, on scenting game so that its master may detect the presence of prey. The pointer "points" by its stance towards the position of the game and the retriever, as one might expect, retrieves shot game from land and also from water.

The job of the spaniel is to flush birds from their cover and to retrieve. The spaniel, however, has undertaken innumerable tasks, and evidence exists that spaniels were being taught to sett as long ago as the 13th century.

Left *The spaniels are descended from Spanish dogs, and are used both to flush out and to retrieve game.*

Above *A sleepy wirehaired pointer belies the alertness demonstrated when it comes "on point," indicating the quarry during a hunt.*

GUNDOG GROUP
Brittany
English Setter
German Shorthaired Pointer
German Wirehaired Pointer
Gordon Setter
Hungarian Vizsla
Irish Red & White Setters
Irish Setter
Italian Spinone
Large Munsterlander
Pointer
Retriever (Chesapeake Bay)
Retriever (Curly Coated)
Retriever (Flat Coated)
Retriever (Golden)
Retriever (Labrador)
Spaniel (American Cocker)
Spaniel (Clumber)
Spaniel (Cocker)
Spaniel (English Springer)
Spaniel (Field)
Spaniel (Irish Water)
Spaniel (Sussex)
Spaniel (Welsh Springer)
Weimaraner

THE HOUND GROUP

Hounds were bred to hunt by sight or scent, hence the terms scent hounds and gaze hounds. Scent hounds, such as the Beagle, Basset and Bloodhound, use their noses to seek their prey. The Afghan Hound, Saluki and Greyhound, to name but a few, are gaze hounds which hunt their prey with the aid of their exceptional sight.

Above Few Basset packs exist today. In the past they were used for hunting hare, and would catch their quarry through persistence rather than speed.

Left The Borzoi is a very swift hound that was used in Russia for wolf-hunting. It hunts by sight rather than scent.

HOUND GROUP

Afghan Hound	Deerhound
Basenji	Elkhound
Basset Fauve De Bretagne	Finnish Spitz
Basset Hound	Greyhound
Beagle	Hamiltonstovare
Bloodhound	Ibizan Hound
Borzoi	Irish Wolfhound
Dachshund (Long-Haired)	Otterhound
Dachshund (Miniature Long-Haired)	Petit Basset Griffon Vendeen
Dachshund (Smooth-Haired)	Pharaoh Hound
Dachshund (Miniature Smooth-Haired)	Rhodesian Ridgeback
Dachshund (Wire-Haired)	Saluki
Dachshund (Miniature Wire-Haired)	Sloughi
	Whippet

There are many hound breeds to choose from, ranging from the Miniature Dachshund to the Greyhound, Bloodhound or Whippet.

With the exception of foxhounds, which inevitably belong to a foxhunting pack, and possibly the Otterhound and Beagle, hounds generally make good household pets. However, they have the instinct to wander, and are unsuitable for those who cannot offer space and a very well-fenced garden.

Bassets in particular have a propensity to roam. Owners have been known to receive telephone calls from many miles distance asking them to come and collect their dog.

Of all the dog types, hounds have the longest association with humans, having been the first to be used by early man for hunting.

POODLE: STANDARD, MINIATURE, TOY

THE GLAMOUR OF THE SHOW Poodle in its elegant lion clip tends to overshadow its versatility. It is a playful, exuberant dog, and a successful competitor in obedience. As a companion, it is intelligent and (particularly the Standard) hardy, and a good retriever. It is also a great imitator which is why Poodles are so often chosen to perform tricks in circuses. They are quick learners.

The Poodle in fact originated as a water retriever and is believed to have evolved from the French Barbet, with its curly woolly coat, and the Hungarian water hound. While it is generally supposed to be a French breed, it originated in Germany, the word Poodle coming from the German "pudelnass" or puddle. In France it is known as the Caniche, this word coming from the French "canard" which means duck. Poodles were great retrievers of duck.

The Miniature and Toy Poodle varieties have of course evolved from the Standard.

The Poodle has Royal connections. "Boy", the inseparable companion of Prince Rupert of the Rhine in the English Civil War (1642–49), was credited with mystical powers. A pamphlet concerning this Poodle is preserved in the Bodleian Library in Oxford, England, and describes how Prince Rupert, with the dog sitting on a table by his side, would frequently during Council debate, turn and kiss it. The dog was killed at the Battle of Marston Moor (1644).

Poodle: Toy

Above The Toy Poodle is descended from the Standard. This example has the black nose, lips, eye rims and nails that are desirable with white or cream coats.

KEY FACTS

Character High spirited and good natured. Excellent show dog.
Exercise Varies with size. The Standard is particularly active. Miniatures and Toys more suitable for town-dwellers.
Grooming Need regular clipping. The lion clip is obligatory for showing. Preparation takes time.
Feeding The Standard would require approximately 1½ cans (400g size) of a branded meaty product, with biscuit added in equal part by volume. (Toy and Miniature, ¼–½ can respectively. But all dogs are individuals!)
Longevity Many poodles live well into their 'teens.
Faults Include eyes set too close together, tail curled, or carried over back.

THE FRENCH CONNECTION

Below The Standard Poodle. The Poodle was once highly valued as a water retriever, although it is seldom used in that role any more.

Varieties: from left to right, black, white, apricot, brown, cream, silver and blue.

The French Queen, Marie Antoinette, is credited with the design of the famous lion clip, which she believed should match the livery of her servants.

Poodles should have almond-shaped eyes and may be any solid colour. However, white and creams should have black nose, lips and eye-rims; black toe-nails are desirable. Apricots should have dark eyes with black points or deep amber eyes with liver points. Blacks, silvers and blues should have black nose, lips, eye-rims and toe-nails, and creams, apricots, browns, silvers and blues may show variations on the same colour up to the age of 18 months.

There is no difference between the three Poodle varieties except in size. Standard: Height at shoulder over 38cm (15in). Miniature: shoulder height at under 38cm (15in) but not under 28cm (11in). Toy: Height at shoulder under 28cm (11in).

THE SHAR-PEI: (CHINESE FIGHTING DOG)

IT IS NOT LONG SINCE the Shar-Pei graced the *Guinness Book of Records* in the World's Rarest Dog slot, but today it has a growing band of devotees in America and Canada, and in the United Kingdom where it is attracting good show entries.

Despite being bred as a fighting dog, the Shar-Pei is an amiable dog unless provoked. Indeed it is believed that drugs were used to promote aggression, while the breed's success as a fighter was largely due to its folds of loose skin, which made it difficult for an adversary to catch hold.

ORIGINS

Likenesses of the Shar-Pei survive from the Han Dynasty (206 BC–AD 220), and it is possible that it originated in Tibet or the northern provinces of China some 2000 years ago.

The future of the Shar-Pei was in peril in 1947, when the People's Republic of China put such a heavy tax on dogs that very few people could keep them. It is fortunate that a number of fine specimens were smuggled out of China.

The dog, which has wrinkles not unlike those of the Bloodhound, stands only 46–51cm (18–20in) at the withers and weighs up to 22.5kg (50lb). It comes in solid colours: black, red, light or dark shades of fawn, and cream.

KEY FACTS

Character Alert, active, calm and independent. Affectionate and devoted.
Exercise Was a wild boar hunter, so needs plenty of it.
Grooming Use fairly stiff brush. Rub down with towel or hound glove.
Feeding Approximately 1½ cans (400g size) of a branded meaty product, with biscuit added in equal part by volume. (Note in all instances: if your dog is over or under the standard weight for its breed, consult your veterinary surgeon.)
Longevity Average.
Faults Include any sign of irritation of eyeball, conjunctiva or eyelids.

Varieties: from top to bottom, fawn, black, red and cream.

THE CHOW CHOW

Varieties: from top to bottom, fawn, black, cream, red, white and blue.

KEY FACTS

Character Beautiful and aloof, this companion and guard reserves its affection for the family.
Exercise It appreciates a fair amount of exercise.
Grooming Use a wire brush, a few minutes daily. An hour-long grooming at weekends works wonders.
Feeding Approximately 1–1½ cans (400g size) of a branded meaty product, with biscuit added in equal part by volume.
Longevity Average.
Faults Include any artificial shortening of the coat which alters the natural outline or expression.

THE BEAUTIFUL CHOW CHOW, with its distinctive blue tongue, is a lion-like member of the Spitz family, known for over 2000 years. It is certainly one of the oldest Spitz and was possibly the original Lama's Mastiff.

This breed had many roles, including those of guard, hunter and sled dog. It was, alas, also bred for its flesh, which is still considered a delicacy in the Far East.

Once known as the Tartar Dog, and also as the Dog of the Barbarians, the Chow Chow has always – rather as the Shar-Pei – had an undeserved reputation for ferocity. It can indeed give a good account of itself, but it is unlikely to pick a fight.

Chow Chows, which have a unique, stilted gait, come in whole-coloured black, red, blue, fawn, cream or white, frequently shaded, but not in patches or parti-coloured (the underpart of tail and back of thighs are frequently of a lighter colour). Dogs stand 48–56cm (19–22in) at shoulder, bitches 46–51cm (18–20in).

SCHNAUZER: GIANT, STANDARD AND MINIATURE

LIKE THE DALMATIAN, Basenji and several other breeds, the Schnauzer gets on well with horses and, in the days of the stage-coach in Central Europe, would run alongside the horses and sleep by the coachman's side at night. It has been used as a messenger in the armed services, is an excellent ratter, and a keen obedience dog. However, the main role of this attractive breed today is as an amusing, intelligent companion. Incidentally, the Miniature Schnauzer was derived from crossing the smallest breed members with another German dog, the Affenpinscher. It is thought that the Schnauzer itself originated by crossing a black German Poodle dog with a grey Spitz.

Above *The Giant Schnauzer, showing pure black markings. It was once used as a cattle dog, and provides an intelligent and playful companion.*

Schnauzer: standard

The Giant Schnauzer, the dog of which stands 65–70cm (25½–27½in) high, and bitches 60–65cm (23½–25½in), was in fact first exhibited in Germany in 1879 under the name Coarsehaired Pinscher ("Pinscher" is German for terrier). In Munich, in October 1909, it was referred to as the Russian-bear Schnauzer, and has been used for policework.

The Standard Schnauzer stands, ideally, 48.5cm (19in) at the withers, and bitches 45.5cm (18in); the Miniature should be 35.5cm (14in), and bitches 33cm (13in).

Schnauzers were first seen in Baden, Württemberg and Bavaria and have long been popular in northern Switzerland and France. They much prefer living indoors, with the family, to life in an outside kennel.

MARKINGS AND COLOURINGS

Colours are: pure black (white markings on head, chest and legs being deemed undesirable) or pepper-and-salt shades ranging from dark iron grey to light grey. The Miniature comes in all pepper-and-salt colours in even proportions, or pure black, or black and silver (solid black with silver markings on eyebrow, muzzle, chest and brisket and on the forelegs below the point of the elbow, on the inside of the hindlegs below the stifle joint, on the vent and under the tail).

KEY FACTS

Character Robust, good with children, playful, yet a fine guard.
Exercise Likes plenty. Will follow horses. Useful obedience dogs.
Grooming Use wire brush daily. Comb whiskers. Coat needs stripping twice a year.
Feeding Miniature: ½–¾ cans (400g size), Standard: 1–1½ cans. Giant: at least 2½ cans of a branded meaty product with biscuit added in equal part by volume.
Longevity Good.
Faults Include any white markings on head, chest and legs.

Varieties: from left to right, black, dark grey, light grey and black and silver.

Left Miniature Schnauzers were created by crossing small Schnauzers with the Affenpinscher. It is less aggressive than the larger varieties.

THE FRENCH BULLDOG

THE "FRENCHIE" has long had a reputation for attaching itself to ladies and it has been the pet of many actresses, writers and ladies of fashion. However, it has no mean number of male devotees who enjoy its companionship and macho image.

BAD TEMPER

Intelligent and devoted, it generally gets on well with other pets, but beware lest its temper should be aroused. A word of reprimand, however, and it will slink away and sulk. The "Frenchie" simply hates to be out of favour!

An ideal companion and show dog – although somewhat heavy to lift on to the show table. They stand at 30-35cm (12-14in); dogs are 12.5kg (28lb) in weight; bitches 11kg (24lb). The development of the breed is generally credited to the French who

KEY FACTS

Character Full of courage, yet with clown-like qualities. Devoted. Intelligent.
Exercise Moderate. Not in very hot weather.
Grooming Use fairly stiff brush daily. Rub down with hound glove or towel. Lubricate facial creases.
Feeding Approximately ¾ can (400g size) of a branded meaty product, with biscuit added in equal part by volume.
Longevity Short to moderate.
Faults Include showing white of eye when looking straight ahead.

are said to have crossed small bulldogs, taken to France by lacemakers from Nottingham, England, in the 19th century, with dogs imported to France from Spain. However, other sources would have it that the French developed the breed by mating a little-known French variety with Belgian imported breeds. In any event, the bat ears and short undocked screwtail are essential features of the breed.

"Frenchies", although not easily obtainable, have a large, enthusiastic band of followers – and rightly so – and always draw an appreciative show audience. They come in brindle, pied or fawn.

Varieties: from left to right, fawn, brindle and pied.

THE DALMATIAN

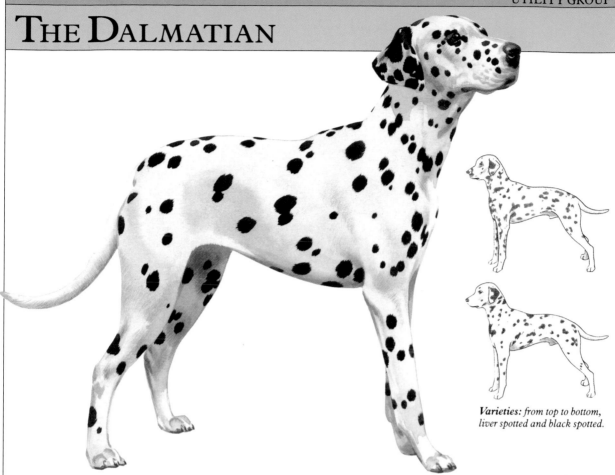

Varieties: from top to bottom, liver spotted and black spotted.

THE DALMATIAN was something of a status symbol in 18th-century England when widely used as a carriage or coach dog. It is generally believed that the breed originated in what is now Yugoslavia, although friezes discovered in Greece and the Middle East depict a similar dog.

THE ALL-PURPOSE DOG

The Dalmatian is a fine all-purpose dog: coach dog, ratter, retriever and draught dog. Today, however, it is mainly kept as a much-loved household pet.

An important point: when buying a Dalmatian puppy, drop a set of keys behind it to test for its reaction. Alas, there is a tendency to deafness in this breed. The desired height of the Dalmatian is 58.4–61cm (23–24in), bitches 55.9–58.4cm (22–23in).

The ground colour is always pure white. Black spotted has dense black spots, and liver spotted, liver brown spots. The spots should not run together, be round, and well distributed.

KEY FACTS

Character Outgoing, friendly. Capable of endurance and speed.
Exercise A traditional coach dog needing plenty of exercise.
Grooming Daily brush and rub down. Easy to care for but beware: neglect grooming and this pet will deposit white hairs on the carpet.
Feeding 1½–2 cans (400g size) of a branded meaty product, with biscuit added in equal part by volume.
Longevity Good.
Faults Include patches, tri-colours and lemon spots. Also bronzing on spots in adults.

THE JAPANESE SPITZ

THE JAPANESE SPITZ is a comparative newcomer outside its native land as both family pet and show dog, and is fast gaining a band of devotees.

To discuss the background of the Japanese Spitz one must look to its close relative the Nordic or Norrbotten Spitz, as they have the same origins.

The breed's ancestor, the Norrbotten Spitz, is also little known outside its native Sweden. It was in fact declared extinct in 1948 but there was renewed interest in the 1960s, resulting in sufficient registrations for the breed to become re-established. These Spitz varieties no doubt derived from Finnish Spitz or Norwegian Buhund ancestry.

The Japanese Spitz was developed as a separate breed in Japan, and is not unlike the Pomeranian (another Spitz variety) but in a larger frame.

The Japanese stands 30–36cm (12–14in), bitches slightly less, and the only allowable colour is pure white. It has a pointed muzzle, triangular ears standing erect, and a bushy tail curled over its back, characteristic of the Spitz breeds.

KEEPING THE SPITZ IN CHECK

This is a sharp little dog, inclined to be yappy if unchecked, perhaps best as the devoted companion of a single person or a couple, rather than with a family and young children.

Above left The Finnish Spitz, one of the Spitz varieties from which the Japanese Spitz is descended. The Spitz dogs have one of the oldest ancestries in the dog world.

Above The Japanese Spitz. It has the long, curly coat characteristic of the Spitz breeds. Pure white is the only acceptable colour.

KEY FACTS

Character Affectionate and companionable, but tends to be wary of strangers.
Exercise A natural herder, enjoys freedom, but will adapt to its owner's requirements.
Grooming Daily with a stiff brush.
Feeding 1 can (400g size) of a branded meaty product, with biscuit added in equal part by volume.
Longevity Good average.
Faults Include ears too wide apart.

Right *The Norwegian Buhund, from which the Japanese Spitz is partly descended, was used as a cattle dog and also makes a good guard dog.*

THE BERNESE MOUNTAIN DOG

THIS BEAUTIFUL ANIMAL is the best known of the four Swiss mountain dogs. The others are the Great Swiss Sennenhund, the Appenzell Sennenhund and the Entlebuch Sennenhund.

In Switzerland Bernese Mountain Dogs are extensively used for draught purposes, and it is not unusual to see a Bernese Mountain Dog pulling milk churns up the mountain side. In some countries (in the United Kingdom, for instance) it is illegal to use dogs in this way, but owners get great enjoyment from harnessing up their pets for off-highway events, such as local fêtes, where they frequently raise money for charity.

A large dog – 64–70cm (25–27½in), bitches 58–66cm (23–26in) – the Bernese is not all that dissimilar to a very large Border Collie. In fact, however, its origins lie in ancient Rome.

Two thousand years ago when Roman legions crossed the Alps into northern Europe they were accompanied by war and guard dogs. From survivors of the latter, four large Alpine breeds evolved, three as sheep herders, the fourth as a draught dog, the Bernese Mountain Dog. It takes its name from Berne from where the inhabitants, many of them weavers, would drive their wares to market in a dog cart.

KEY FACTS

Character A multi-purpose farm dog, capable of draught work. An ideal family pet in the right environment.
Exercise This is not a town dog. It needs plenty of exercise.
Grooming Regular brushing or coat will shed.
Feeding Approximately 2 cans (400g size) of a branded meaty product, with biscuit added in equal part by volume.
Longevity Average.
Faults Any sign of aggression, which must not be tolerated.

Above The Pyrenean Mountain Dog is immensely powerful and at one time was *used in battle. Today, however, it is known for its gentle, loyal nature.*

THE OUTDOOR LIFE

The Bernese makes an excellent family pet in the right environment. It needs space and exercise. It would be cruel to keep it in an apartment. It also prefers cold weather and while many breed members do live indoors they come to no harm being kennelled outside.

The breed tends to devote itself to one person, but will adapt to share its tremendous loyalty with the family.

The coat of the Bernese should be jet black, with rich reddish brown on cheeks, over the eyes, and on all four legs and chest. There is a slight to medium-sized symmetrical white head marking (blaze) and white chest marking (cross) which are essential. White paws are preferred, but are not essential.

THE ROTTWEILER

THE ROTTWEILER is a splendid animal which in recent times has received adverse publicity, largely through breed members having fallen into unsuitable, inexperienced hands.

The Rottweiler has been known since the Middle Ages, when it was a hunter of wild boar, and has developed into a trusted cattle dog. It comes from the German town of Rottweil in Württemberg where – known as the Rottweiler Metzgerhund or Rottweil Butcher's Dog – it was frequently used for draught purposes and would pull the butchers' carts. It has also been used as a police dog and guard in the armed services.

A LOYAL COMPANION

The Rottweiler is a natural guard and protector and extremely loyal to its master, and its master's family – and other pets – if it has been brought up with them. It does however require knowledgeable handling and obedience training, and to provoke it into aggression is sheer stupidity bearing in mind the strength of this dog, and the fact that it rarely gives any warning of attack.

Sadly too much emphasis has been placed on the breed's macho image and too little on its abilities as, for example, sled dog, mountain rescue dog and

KEY FACTS

Character Bold, courageous and loyal. Working dog and guard. Not recommended for the inexperienced.
Exercise This former wild boar hunter and cattle dog needs an outlet for its energies.
Grooming Regular brushing.
Feeding Approximately 2–2 ½ cans (400g size) of a branded meaty product, with biscuit added in equal part by volume.
Longevity Average.
Faults Fearsome, if provoked.

Above The Rottweiler should be black with markings that range from tan to mahogany in colour.

Right The Rottweiler is a former hunting dog that is widely used by the police and armed services. Here, a dog is being trained for police duties.

obedience competitor.

The Rottweiler stands 63–69cm (25–27in) high, bitches 58–63.5cm (23–25in). Its colour is always black with clearly defined markings including a spot over each eye. Markings range from rich tan to mahogany and should not exceed 10% of body colour.

THE GREAT DANE

THE MAGNIFICENT GREAT DANE is slow to anger and good with children and other pets. However, because of its sheer size, it is boisterous when young and needs disciplining if it is not to get the upper hand. A weekly visit to the dog training club with this breed would be time well invested.

Acknowledged as a German breed, the Great Dane is believed to be a descendant of the Molossus hounds of Roman times. These were dogs that hunted wild boar, baited bulls and acted as bodyguards, but there is little of this aggression apparent in the present-day Dane.

THE "APOLLO OF THE DOG WORLD"

Bismarck (1815–98), who had a penchant for the Mastiff, took an interest in the breed and produced a Dane similar to the type we know today by crossing the Mastiff of southern Germany with the Great

Above *This Great Dane has a fawn coat, one of several colour varieties.*

Varieties: *from left to right, fawn, blue, harlequin, black and brindle.*

Left *The Neapolitan Mastiff's ancestry can be traced back 2500 years. It is an effective guard dog.*

Great Dane

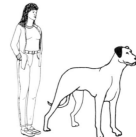

Character Devoted, good natured and easy to train – but not cheap to feed!
Exercise Ideally, miles of walking on hard ground every day, if you haven't the land to give it freedom.
Grooming Daily grooming with a body brush.
Feeding Up to 4 cans (400g size) of a branded meaty product, with biscuit added in equal part by volume.
Longevity Short. Average eight or nine years.
Faults A little boisterous when young. Any roughness in coat.

Dane of the north. This dog was first exhibited at Hamburg in 1863 and by 1866 it had become known as the Deutsche Dogge and was referred to as the National Dog of Germany. It is often called the "Apollo of the dog world".

The minimum size of a Great Dane over 18 months of age should be 76cm (30in), bitches 71cm (28in). There are a number of colours including brindle, fawn, blue, black and the distinctive harlequin (a pure white underground with all-black or all-blue patches).

One of the saddest things about owning a Great Dane is the knowledge that it has only a short life-span, for those that attain eight or nine years have done well, and in their latter years they have a tendency to suffer from heart complaints and stiff joints. However, such is the devotion that many owners have for this breed that they feel even a few years are worth while.

THE DOBERMAN

THE DOBERMAN was bred as a fiercesome guard. Indeed Louis Dobermann of Apolda in Thuringia, Germany, the man from whom the breed took its name, was a tax collector in the 1880s with a penchant for fierce dogs. He wanted the ideal animal to accompany him on his rounds, not a difficult task as he was keeper of the local dog pound, with access to innumerable strays. Intent on breeding for courage, alertness and stamina, Dobermann introduced the Rottweiler to the German Pinscher, and (it is believed) the Manchester Terrier as well, and possibly even the Pointer.

Despite its strong guarding instincts, and provided it receives sufficient training, the Doberman can become a reliable family pet. It is a good tracker, police dog and just the animal to have guarding a stables or small-holding.

The Doberman stands 69cm (27in), bitches 65cm (25½in), and comes in definite black, brown, blue or fawn (Isabella) only, with rust red markings. Incidentally, white markings of any kind are highly undesirable.

Left The Doberman is a loyal and devoted pet, and has very strong guarding instincts.

Below It can be black, as here, brown, blue or fawn, with rust markings.

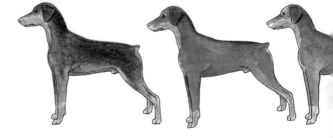

KEY FACTS

Character An alert, aloof guard. Loyal and devoted to owner.
Exercise The ideal dog for a stable yard or environment offering unfettered freedom.
Grooming Daily rubdown with turkish towelling. This will remove surplus hairs.
Feeding Approximately 1½–2½ cans (400g size) of a branded meaty product, with biscuit added in equal part by volume.
Longevity Good.
Faults Include a possible tendency to overguard.

Right *The Doberman probably contains some Manchester Terrier blood in its ancestry.*

Varieties: *from left to right, black, brown, blue and fawn.*

THE SIBERIAN HUSKY

KEY FACTS

Character Reliable, medium-sized working sled dog.
Exercise This dog has considerable endurance and a great turn of speed. Not suitable for the suburban semi.
Grooming Daily brushing and combing. Towelling after coat has got wet. Coat sheds once a year, when surplus hair will need combing out.
Feeding 1½–2½ cans (400g size) of a branded meaty product, with biscuit added in equal part by volume.
Longevity Good average.
Faults Include a tendency to wander. Can be destructive.

Top *The Alaskan Malamute, like the Husky, is a Spitz breed. It is stronger than the Husky and can pull heavier loads.*

Above *A Siberian Husky pup. Huskies are tireless, willing workers and make devoted companions.*

CAPABLE OF GREAT SPEED AND ENDURANCE, the Siberian Husky is a medium-sized working sled dog with a long history of friendship with man. It is also good with children. However, it is a breed which needs space and training if it is not to wander off and molest livestock or become destructive.

This is a dog that will not refuse to leave the fireside in wintertime. In fact, the colder it is the better for this animal. It was bred by the nomadic Chukchi tribes of north-east Asia with the aim of producing a hardy dog which could combine the roles of companion and hunter with that of a speedy sled dog.

It now draws appreciative audiences at dog shows, is used as a Search and Rescue dog and is linked world-wide with the sport of sled dog racing.

It originated from the Kolyma River region of Siberia, which extends eastward to the Bering Strait, and was first imported into Alaska in 1909.

The Siberian Husky weighs in at 20–27kg (45–60lb), bitches 16–23kg (35–50lb). Comes in all colours and markings, including white. A variety of markings on the head are common and include many striking patterns not found in other breeds.

This is a dog which does not display aggression towards strangers or, indeed, other dogs, but is somewhat reserved in maturity; dogs stand 53–60cm (21–23½ in), and bitches 51–56cm (20–22 in).

Right Samoyed puppies showing the famous 'Samoyed smile'. The Samoyed is a happy, friendly, intelligent breed, popular in obedience tests and in the show ring.

Varieties: top from left to right, black and white, silver grey and white and black and tan: bottom from left to right, white, grey and white and fawn.

THE NEWFOUNDLAND

A GENTLE GIANT, capable of hard work, but suitable as a house pet as long as there is sufficient space. The Newfoundland gets along well with other pets, and may be kept even with toy varieties.

Just as the Border Collie has the natural instinct to round up anything that moves, the Newfoundland has the instinct to swim out to sea and rescue anything in the water, swimming back with it safely to shore.

The breed originates from the north-east of Canada, into whose harbours fishing boats would frequently arrive to avoid bad weather. It is thought that such ships' dogs mated with local dogs whose ancestors included native American dogs and Basque sheepdogs, to produce the Newfoundland.

This is the dog beloved of the poet Byron, whose Newfoundland "Boatswain" is buried in the grounds of his former home, Newstead Abbey. It also became famous through the paintings of Sir Edward Landseer (1802–73) from whom the Landseer variety, with black and white markings, take their name.

The average height of the Newfoundland is 71cm (28in), bitches 66cm (26in), while their weight is 64–68kg (140–150lb), bitches 50–54kg (110–120lb).

Colours permitted are black, brown and "Landseer".

KEY FACTS

Character Excellent guard, fine swimmer, marvellous with children and other animals.
Exercise Regular exercise on hard ground.
Grooming Daily brushing with a hard brush.
Feeding At least 2½ cans (400g size) of a branded meaty product, with biscuit added in equal part by volume.
Longevity Average.
Faults Include tails with a kink, or curled over back.

Varieties: from left to right, black, brown and Landseer.

THE MASTIFF

THE MASTIFF is an ancient and powerful guard dog, already found in Britain when Julius Caesar landed in 55 BC. It is said that, at that time, the Mastiff was fighting alongside his British masters. Thereafter the Romans took a number of these powerful dogs back with them to fight in the arenas of Rome.

There are, however, sources which credit the Mastiff with Eastern origin, believing that its ancestry traces back to Tibetan Mastiffs.

It should be noted that the Mastiff is an entirely different breed from the Bull Mastiff, which is a cross between a Mastiff and an English Bulldog. The Mastiff is the larger of the two.

The Mastiff, as a former guard dog and war dog, was undoubtedly bred for violence. This has been bred out so that today the Mastiff is a brave and friendly companion, good with children, albeit sometimes wary with strangers. However, it is not a "beginner's dog" and it would be foolish with a

KEY FACTS

Character Brave, intelligent and loyal.
Exercise Needs plenty. Best kept on a farm or estate.
Grooming Daily brushing.
Feeding 2½–4 cans (400g size) of a branded meaty product, with biscuit added in equal part by volume.
Longevity Average.
Faults Include a tendency to lameness. Check with veterinarian for soundness.

dog of this size not to invest considerable time in training.

The Mastiff stands 76cm (30in), bitches 70cm (27½in). Colours are apricot-fawn, silver-fawn, or dark fawn brindle. In all cases, muzzle, ears, eyes and nose should be black with round orbits, with the black extending upwards between them.

Varieties: from top to bottom, fawn, brindle and silver.

THE BOXER

FOR THE FAMILY with young children, the boxer is an excellent choice. It is fairly exuberant, and takes a long time to grow up, but generally fits in well with the average family, particularly if there is someone able to take it for long country walks. However, in summer it should not be taken for walks in the heat of the day. Boxers can also be trained for obedience and have been used by the police, in the armed forces and as Guide Dogs for the Blind.

The Boxer's ancestry goes back to the "holding" dogs of Molossus (Mastiff) type, taken into battle against the wild Cimbrians by the Romans. The jaw, like that of the Bulldog, is undershot – a common trait in bull baiters. The Brabant bull-baiter, from which the English Bulldog evolved, also had a hand in the evolution of the Boxer.

The Boxer stands 57–63cm (22½–25in), bitches 53–59cm (21–23in) and comes in fawn or brindle. The all-white Boxer, which makes an attractive pet, is unacceptable in the show ring. The ears are cropped in many countries.

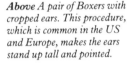

Above A pair of Boxers with cropped ears. This procedure, which is common in the US and Europe, makes the ears stand up tall and pointed.

Left Boxers are descended from the mastiffs, such as the Bull Mastiff, which has the characteristic undershot jaw and powerful body.

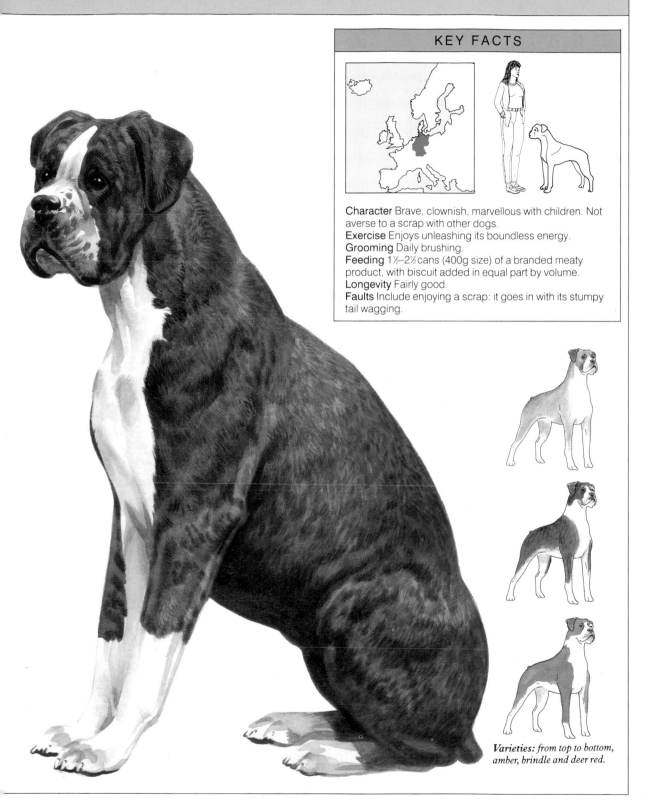

Character Brave, clownish, marvellous with children. Not averse to a scrap with other dogs.
Exercise Enjoys unleashing its boundless energy.
Grooming Daily brushing.
Feeding 1½–2½ cans (400g size) of a branded meaty product, with biscuit added in equal part by volume.
Longevity Fairly good.
Faults Include enjoying a scrap: it goes in with its stumpy tail wagging.

Varieties: from top to bottom, amber, brindle and deer red.

THE ST BERNARD

THIS GENTLE GIANT makes an ideal family pet for those with the room to accommodate it. Care must, however, be taken to select a St Bernard pup from a kennel renowned for producing stock both free of hip dysplasia (to which the breed is prone) and with the good temperament for which it is renowned.

The breed takes its name from the refuge of St Bernard in the Alps founded shortly before the year AD 1000 by a young nobleman, Bernard de Menthon. Its purpose was to give shelter to travellers over the pass, and those who might have become buried in the snow.

Left The Anatolian Sheepdog
is agile and strong. It is easy to
train, but is suspicious of
strangers, making it a good
guard dog.

Varieties: from left to right,
orange, mahogany and brindle.

Left The Anatolian Sheepdog
is agile and strong. It is easy to
train, but is suspicious of
strangers, making it a good
guard dog.

Varieties: from left to right,
orange, mahogany and brindle.

Right The Estrela Mountain
Dog is tough and rugged.
Although calm with its owner,
it is not good with strangers.
Although originally a sheep
dog, it also makes a good guard
dog.

Following Bernard's death the refuge continued
to offer hospitality, but it was not until the middle
of the 17th century that the monks, who by then ran
the refuge, made the decision to enlist the aid of
dogs capable of withstanding the rigours of the Alps
to rescue travellers.

Some sources credit the monks with having
crossed German Mastiffs with Pyrenean Mountain
Dogs to create the St Bernard. More likely, it is a
descendant of the Tibetan Mastiff.

The breed faced extinction around 1820, but a
dedicated band of dog fanciers continued breeding
and were successful in producing the fine dog we
know today.

There are, in fact, two types of St Bernard: long-
haired and short-haired. The monks concentrated
on short-haired stock, because snow can gather in
long hair and form heavy icicles, impeding the
dogs' work.

BIG IS BEAUTIFUL

Because of their sheer size – there is no standard
laid down but the taller they are, the better in show
terms, provided symmetry is maintained – and
resultant feeding costs, one does not see too many
St Bernards, but those one does see are generally of
good quality.

The colour of the St Bernard may be orange,
mahogany, brindle (or red-brindle), white with
patches on body of any of the aforementioned
colours. Markings are white muzzle, white blaze on
face, white collar, white chest, white forelegs, feet

KEY FACTS

Character Calm, sensible, trustworthy and courageous.
Mountain rescue dog.
Exercise Plenty. However, not too much before adulthood.
Grooming Regular combing and brushing to keep coat in
good condition and avoid shedding.
Feeding At least 2½ cans (400g size) of a branded meaty
product, with biscuit added in equal part by volume.
Longevity Not long-lived.
Faults Chest should never project below elbows. Subject
to hip deformities.

and end of tail, black shadings on face and ears.

Often told is the story of Barry, a breed member
at the famous hospice which, between 1800 and
1810, is credited with saving no less than forty lives.
However, the St Bernard tends to be associated by
most people with a famous brand of brandy, which
for many years they have been used to advertise.

THE KOMONDOR

KEY FACTS

Character Excellent guard, wary of strangers. Not for the inexperienced, but immensely loyal to owner.

Exercise Puppies are particularly active. Adults need a good amount of exercise, which must be on a lead if in town.

Grooming The Komondor has a thick double coat. The undercoat is soft and woolly, the outer coat long, coarse and wavy. The coat forms in tassel-like cords which are never brushed and combed, although matting has to be avoided.

Feeding At least 2½ cans (400g size) of a branded meaty product, with biscuit added in equal part by volume.

Longevity Good.

Faults Include erect or partially erect ears.

THE KOMONDOR – the plural in Hungarian is Komondorok – is a large, white dog that looks like a dish-mop. It has been bred in its native Hungary for over 1000 years, and is one of the world's best guard dogs, bred to guard flocks and possessions. It will also protect your children and other livestock with its life. However, it does not take to strangers too kindly and is best in a country environment. Also, while it will live happily indoors, it is ideally suited to an outdoor kennel, its corded coat rendering it impervious to the cold.

Dogs average 80cm (31½in) high, bitches average 70cm (27½in). The colour is always white. Ideally the skin is grey, but pink skin is acceptable.

THE OLD ENGLISH SHEEPDOG

KEY FACTS

Character Great stamina and sound temperament. Gets on well with children and other animals.
Exercise Plenty. Good garden essential for this boisterous breed.
Grooming Daily brushing. Comb with steel comb. Lengthy show preparation.
Feeding Approximately 2½ cans (400g size) of a branded meaty product, with biscuit added in equal part by volume.
Longevity Average.
Faults Include light eyes.

Varieties: from left to right, grey, grizzle and blue.

"BOBTAIL" or the Old English Sheepdog is thought to have resulted from the crossing of the Briard with the large Russian Owtscharka, which is related to Hungarian sheepdogs. It was once used in England as cattle dog and guard. Nowadays it is kept almost solely as a family pet, and while it is a good-natured dog, it is not always a good choice for the suburban home because of its sheer bulk and exuberance.

Indeed, over-popularity in Britain following the breed's appearance in a television commercial has resulted in rescue societies being inundated with requests from owners wanting a home found for "Bobtails" which they bought on impulse and found too large to cope with in an apartment, or to exercise alongside a pram. But in the right environment it is a first-rate companion, devoted and sensible and good with children.

Standing 61cm (24in) or more, bitches 56cm (22in) or more, the "Bobtail" comes in any shade of grey, grizzle or blue. Body and hindquarters of solid colour with or without white socks.

THE WELSH CORGI: PEMBROKE AND CARDIGAN

THE WELSH CORGI CARDIGAN is one of Britain's most ancient breeds, brought over from the continent by the Celts more than 3000 years ago. It is thought to originate from the same stock as the German Basset Hound. It has worked in Wales since the 11th century and is mentioned in Domesday Book which was instigated by William the Conqueror. Its traditional role was always to move cattle by nipping at their ankles, a habit for which it is famous, as the servants and staff of Queen Elizabeth II know to their cost.

The Welsh Corgi Pembroke came over in the company of Flemish weavers who were summoned by Henry I in 1107 to introduce their craft into Wales. The Pembroke is related to various Nordic dogs such as the Samoyed and Norwegian Elkhound.

The two Corgis only began to resemble each other in the middle of the nineteenth century when the two types were crossed. The Pembroke is taller and shorter in the body than the Cardigan which is instantly recognizable by its foxy tail.

The Welsh Corgi Cardigan stands 30cm (12in) at the shoulder and may be any colour, with or without white markings. White should not predominate.

The Welsh Corgi Pembroke stands 25.4–30.5cm (10–12in) at the shoulder. Colours are self in red, sable, fawn, black-and-tan with or without white markings on legs, brisket and neck. Some white on head and foreface is allowed.

A word of warning: don't allow your pet Corgi to jump on and off chairs if it is overweight, or this could result in back problems.

A popular pet, the Corgi is also a great favourite with the show ring fraternity.

Pembroke varieties: from left to right, sable, black and tan, red and fawn.

Welsh Corgi (Pembroke)

Cardigan varieties: from left to right, fawn and white, black and white, red and white, sable, tan, brown and black.

Left *The Cardigan Corgi is a very ancient breed that originated in Europe. In the past it was used as a cattle dog. This type of coat is known as blue merle, a mixture of grey, black and blue hair.*

Below *The Pembroke Corgi is longer in the leg and shorter in the body than the Cardigan. The two Corgis were recognized as separate breeds in Britain in 1934.*

KEY FACTS

Character Devoted companion, tireless worker and fine guard.
Exercise Despite its traditional role as a worker, will settle for regular walks. Don't neglect these or the Corgi will lose its waistline.
Grooming Daily brushing is all that is needed for this breed's water-resistant coat.
Feeding Approximately ¾ can (400g size) of a branded meaty product, with biscuit added in equal part by volume.
Longevity Good average.
Faults Inherent tendency to nip. The Cardigan has the slightly quieter temperament.

THE GERMAN SHEPHERD DOG

Varieties: from left to right, black and gold, black, grey, black and tan, white.

ONE OF THE MOST POPULAR DOGS in the world, the German Shepherd has been attributed to the Bronze Age wolf, and, indeed, around the 7th century AD, a sheepdog of this type, but with a lighter coat, existed in Germany. By the 16th century the coat had darkened.

First exhibited in Hanover in 1882, the German Shepherd was introduced into the United Kingdom after the First World War by a band of dedicated fanciers who had seen the breed working in Germany. However, at that time it was considered inappropriate to glorify a breed with a Germanic name and it therefore became known not as the German Shepherd, but the Alsatian, not reverting to its original and correct name, until 1971. There are many today who still refer to the breed as the Alsatian.

The German Shepherd is undoubtedly one of the most intelligent of breeds. It has fought valiantly in wars, been used as a Guide Dog for the Blind, police and Search and Rescue Dog and successful obedience competitor.

LOVE AND TRAINING

Sadly, the reputation this breed has for ferocity is largely due to breed members falling into the wrong hands. The bored, restless, nervous German

KEY FACTS

Character Versatile and alert working dog with keen scenting ability. Excellent guard.
Exercise Needs plenty. Best to channel its keen intelligence and exuberance into tasks such as obedience or agility.
Grooming Daily brushing.
Feeding 1½–2½ cans (400g size) of a branded meaty product, with biscuit added in equal part by volume.
Longevity Good average.
Faults Include a possible tendency to overguard.

Above The Groenendael is the most popular of the varieties of Belgian Shepherd Dog.

Shepherd can indeed be dangerous. However, the dog that is carefully trained, loved, and given a task to do which will satisfy its boundless energy and keen intelligence should have no problems.

The German Shepherd is a faithful defender of any children in the family, trouble only arising when, for example, it might misinterpret a move towards a child in its care.

The German Shepherd is constantly "on guard", noting any move on the part of a visitor which might constitute a threat to its beloved family. Teaching this breed to be aggressive is sheer stupidity. The instinct to defend should the need arise is inbuilt.

Sadly, the GSD, as it is affectionately called, is subject to hip dysplasia, malformation of the ball of the hip joint, which can result in chronic lameness before middle age. Because of this, and the fact that the breed's great popularity has caused the commercially minded to breed from poor stock, it is all the more important to select a breeding kennel with great care.

Standing 62.5cm (25in), bitches 57.5cm (23in), allowable colours are black or black saddle with tan, or gold to light grey markings. All-black, all-grey, or grey with lighter or brown markings are referred to as Sables. The white German Shepherd, although widely used by the armed forces, and with a growing band of devotees, is not recognized by the United Kingdom Kennel Club.

Left The German Shepherd is a direct descendant of the wolf. It is constantly on the alert, ready to protect its family, and benefits from being given obedience or agility tasks to perform to keep it occupied.

THE BORDER COLLIE

THE BORDER COLLIE (the term "Border" refers to the border country of England, Scotland and Wales) has become almost a folk hero through its television appearances at sheepdog trials and obedience competitions. A hardy, working sheepdog it is also the undoubted favourite of the obedience trainers and has, not all that wisely, been increasingly taken into suburban homes in the role of family pet. A natural herder (anything from pigs to people), the home is perhaps not the best environment for this worker which, while it has a fondness for children, can become bored and snappy through lack of exercise, freedom and space.

The present day Border Collies are a modern strain descended from collies of the Lowland and Border counties of England and Scotland. They are working sheepdogs of a distinct, recognizable type and have been exported, often at great cost, to many countries of the world.

The ideal height of the Border Collie is 53cm (21in), bitches slightly less, and a variety of colours are permissible, although white should never be the predominant colour.

A young Border Collie will crouch instinctively in the presence of sheep. Farmers generally get an older working Collie to teach them their paces.

Below *The Rough Collie comes from the lowlands of Scotland, where it has a long history as a herding dog.*

Right *The Smooth Collie, because of its lack of a thick coat, shows the athletic shape of the collies.*

Varieties: a variety of markings are permissible, but white should never predominate.

Right *Another native of Scotland, the Bearded Collie is an intelligent and lively dog that loves plenty of exercise.*

KEY FACTS

Character Tenacious, hardworking sheepdog of great tractability. Not suitable for suburban environment.
Exercise Ample if it is not to become bored and snappy.
Grooming Brush with an equine dandy brush. Remove dead fur after grooming.
Feeding 1–1½ cans (400g size) of a branded meaty product, with biscuit added in equal part by volume.
Longevity Good average.
Faults Include any tendency to coarseness or weediness.

THE GRIFFON: BRUXELLOIS AND BRABACON

THE GRIFFON comes in two varieties: the rough (Griffon Bruxellois) and the smooth, more correctly known as the Griffon Brabançon. In the USA the breed is referred to as the Brussels Griffon.

The Griffon is an affectionate, intelligent, happy little dog, with an almost human expression. It revels in being with its owner and will follow for miles, whether picking up driftwood on a beach, or walking sedately in the park. However, while they have the facility to follow, they are not the easiest of breeds to lead-train. Perseverance is the key.

Generally good natured with children and other pets, the Griffon is an excellent house dog, but does have the tendency to yap if unchecked. Like other short-nosed breeds, great care must be taken that it

KEY FACTS

Character Hardy, happy, intelligent and devoted.
Exercise Adaptable. Not too keen on lead. Will follow for miles, or settle for a walk in the park.
Grooming Rough coat needs stripping, smooth coat needs brushing, towelling and rubbing down with chamois leather.
Feeding Approximately ½ can (400g size) of a branded meaty product, with biscuit added in equal part by volume.
Longevity Long lived.
Faults Include high stepping front movement.

Varieties: from left to right, black and tan, black and red.

Above *A Rough-coated Griffon, or Griffon Bruxellois. Black and tan is one of three colour varieties. The Rough's coat needs regular attention.*

does not become overheated in warm weather, that there is adequate ventilation and drinking water.

Whether to choose the rough- or smooth-coated variety is a matter of personal inclination. Roughs seem to come away with more prizes in the show ring, perhaps because of their sheer numbers, but their coats do need a fair amount of attention.

Sometimes referred to as "the mongrel of the pure-bred dog world" the Griffon is said to derive from the Affenpinscher, while the smooth-coat undoubtedly owes much to the Pug.

A ROYAL FAVOURITE

Once used in stables to kill vermin, the Griffon was first exhibited at the Brussels Exhibition in 1880. Later it found immense popularity when the much-loved Queen Astrid of the Belgians took a fancy to the breed though numbers were severely reduced during the war years (1940–45).

Today the Griffon is loved and exhibited in many countries of the world.

The Griffon weighs from 2.2–5kg (5–11lb), 2.7–4.5kg (6–10lb) most desirable, and comes in clear red, black or black-and-rich-tan, without white markings.

Above *The Smooth-coated, or Griffon Brabaçon. Its face clearly shows its Pug ancestry.*

Griffon: Bruxellois

THE AFFENPINSCHER

KEY FACTS

Character Lively, loving and self-confident. Carries itself with comic seriousness.
Exercise Adaptable to town or country. Enjoys a walk.
Grooming Regular trimming, daily brushing.
Feeding Approximately ½ can (400g size) of a branded meaty product, with biscuit added in equal part by volume.
Longevity Good.
Faults Include hackneyed action.

THIS DOG, with its monkey-like appearance, is well named. The Affenpinscher is a German breed, and the word "Affe" is German for monkey. Indeed the Germans often call this little dog the Zwergaffenpinscher – "Zwerg" meaning dwarf – while the French call it the "moustached devil". It is the smallest of the Schnauzers and Pinschers, but would do battle with a lion if roused!

Until 1896, Miniature Pinschers and Affenpinschers were classified as one breed. In that year, however, it was decreed that the long-coats should thereafter be known as Affenpinschers and they were shown as such at the Berlin Show.

In fact the Affenpinscher has been in Germany at least since the Middle Ages, and is included in famous paintings by Jan van Eyck (1395–1441) and Albrecht Dürer (1471–1528). However, despite this strong Germanic connection controversy exists as to whether, as is supposed, it contributed to the Griffon Bruxellois, or the other way round.

A comic, lovable little fellow with a mind of its own, the Affenpinscher, which is black, sometimes with grey shading, stands 24–28cm (9½–11in) tall and weighs 3–4kg (6½– 9lb).

THE CHINESE CRESTED DOG

KEY FACTS

Character Happy, never vicious, extremely energetic and affectionate.

Exercise Enjoys a walk but tends to exercise itself rushing about in the home.

Grooming Bathing about every three weeks, and skin treated with baby cream. Crest and tail plume brushed. Shave off any stray hairs for show.

Feeding Rapacious appetite but averagely ½–¾ can (400g size) of a branded meaty product, with biscuit added in equal part by volume.

Longevity Average.

Faults Include light eyes. They should be so dark as to appear black.

THE CHINESE CRESTED DOG was almost extinct until, in 1966, Mrs Ruth Harris of Gloucestershire in England contacted an elderly lady in the United States who owned the only remaining examples of the breed. Mrs Harris imported several of these. The breed is kept both for the show ring and as household pets.

Varieties: from top to bottom, brown spotted, blue, black spotted, silver grey.

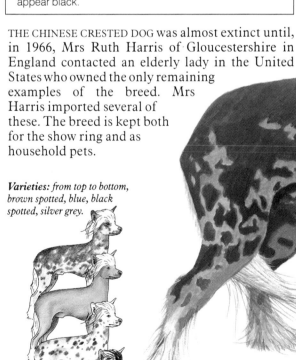

"POWDER PUFFS"

Happy and scatty, the Chinese Crested is an extremely active little dog which simply cannot resist the temptation to use a room as a race circuit. It is, however, lovable, reasonably intelligent, good natured and usually fairly easy to train to the lead. Strange but true is that haired examples of the breed, known as Powder Puffs, appear in almost every litter, and are thought to be nature's way of keeping the other, hairless, pups warm.

The Chinese Crested comes in two distinct body types: the Deer, which is racy and fine-boned, and the Cobby, which is heavier in body and bone. It stands 28–33cm (11–13in) at withers, bitches 23–30cm (9–12in). Weight varies considerably but should not be over 5.5kg (12lb).

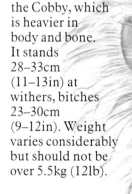

THE YORKSHIRE TERRIER

SO POPULAR has the Yorkshire Terrier become that there are many specimens about in varying sizes. The unknowledgeable will tell you that their pet is, or isn't a 'miniature'. In fact the standard for the breed calls for a dog up to 3kg (7lb) in weight, that is only 450g (1lb) more than the standard for the world's smallest dog, the Chihuahua. However, there is no doubt that some of the bigger Yorkies one sees around do make happy, hardy pets.

With its keen terrier temperament in a small frame, the Yorkie makes a first-rate companion, and will live happily whether in an apartment or a farm. However, the show specimen tends to live a

KEY FACTS

Character Alert, intelligent terrier in a small frame.
Exercise Will walk its owner literally off his/her feet in the country, or settle for a walk in the park.
Grooming Daily brushing and combing for the pet owner. Continuous work for the show aspirant.
Feeding Approximately ½ can (400g size) of a branded meaty product, with biscuit added in equal part by volume.
Longevity The 16-year-old Yorkie is not a rarity, but obviously there is no hard and fast rule.
Faults Described as the tyrant of the dog world, it may well take you over, with your household, if unchecked.

Above The Maltese Terrier is one of the oldest dog breeds. Records of it go back at least to Roman times.

Right The Yorkie's coat should be dark steel blue, with a rich tan colour across the chest. It needs daily grooming to keep it looking its best.

sedate life, spending most of its time done up in rag-like paper curlers.

The origin of this little dog is fairly new. Its ancestry traces back only about 100 years to the crossing of a Skye Terrier with the old Black and Tan Terrier. Rumour has it that the Maltese Terrier and even the Dandie Dinmont, may also have played a part.

The Yorkie, whose coat should hang quite straight and evenly down each side, with a parting extending from nose to end of tail, should be dark steel blue in colour (not silver blue), extending from occiput to roof of tail, never mingled with fawn, bronze or dark hairs. The hair on its chest should be a rich, bright tan, and all tan hair must be darker at the roots than in the middle, shading still lighter at the tips.

THE POMERANIAN

Varieties: from top to bottom, white, brown, orange, blue, beaver, cream and black.

THE POMERANIAN, once Queen Victoria's favourite until ousted by the Imperial Pekingese, is often wrongly thought of as the lap dog of elderly ladies. It lends itself well to that role, but is well equipped to tackle a country walk with its owner.

The breed, which is reckoned to be of European origin, takes its name from Pomerania. However, being a small Spitz it is more than likely that its beginnings were in the Arctic Circle. It was, in any case, a much larger dog, up to 13.6kg (30lb) in weight before being bred down; until in 1896 shows were divided into classes for Poms over and under that weight. Since 1915, the over 3.6kg (8lb) variety has been eliminated.

The Pomeranian, with its foxy head and intelligent expression, comes in a whole variety of colours, but must be free from black or white shadings. Whole colours are white, black, brown, light or dark blue (as pale as possible), orange (as self-coloured and bright as possible), beaver, and cream. Creams have black noses and black eye-rims. Whites must be quite free from lemon or any other colour.

KEY FACTS

Character Happy, hardy and devoted. Thinks it is a much bigger dog.

Exercise Some Poms are exercised in the garden or park, others go for long walks in the countryside with their owners.

Grooming Plenty of time needed to care for the Pom's double coat, a short, fluffy under-coat and a long, straight top coat. Daily brushing with stiff brush. Regular trimming.

Feeding Approximately ½ can (400g size) of a branded meaty product, with biscuit added in equal part by volume.

Longevity Many live into their 'teens.

Faults Include eyes set too wide apart.

THE MINIATURE PINSCHER

THE DELIGHTFUL Miniature Pinscher (commonly known as the "Min Pin") is not, as many suppose, a bred-down version of the Doberman. It is a much older breed, a descendant of the German Smooth-haired Pinscher to which the Dachshund and Italian Greyhound probably contributed.

The Min Pin is a high-stepping little dog, a natural showman, and a joy to watch. It has, however, got a mind of its own and, in common with many small breeds, is likely to yap if unchecked. It is so attractive that most owners let their Min Pins get away with murder.

KEY FACTS

Character Fearless, self possessed and spirited. Intelligent and easy to look after.
Exercise Suitable for town and country and will adapt to its owner's needs.
Grooming Daily brush and rub down with a chamois leather.
Feeding Approximately ½ can (400g size) of a branded meaty product, with biscuit added in equal part by volume.
Longevity Good average.
Faults Include hocks which turn in or out.

Standing from 25.5–30cm (10–12in) at withers, the Miniature Pinscher may be black, blue, chocolate with sharply defined tan markings, or solid red.

It did, incidentally, receive pure-bred (pedigree) status in 1895 from the German Pinscher-Schnauzer Klub.

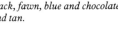

Varieties: from top to bottom, black, fawn, blue and chocolate and tan.

113

THE PEKINGESE

KEY FACTS

Character Aloof, dignified, small well-balanced dog of quality.
Exercise Despite its glamorous appearance in the show ring, the Pekingese enjoys nothing better than a good long scamper in the mud. Park walks will, however, suffice.
Grooming Daily brushing with a soft-bristled brush. Best to tackle the under-side with the Peke lying on its back.
Feeding Approximately ½ can (400g size) of a branded meaty product, with biscuit added in equal part by volume.
Longevity Can live well into the 'teens.
Faults Include domed skull.

THE PEKINGESE always seems aware of its regal background. In fact, it came to the West after 1860 when British troops looted and burned the Summer Palace at Peking. Five Pekingese were found in the women's apartments and taken back to England. Nicknamed "Looty", one was presented to Queen Victoria and became a great favourite, being painted by the artist Landseer.

DEVOTED DOGS

The Peke may not receive the same devotion as when slave girls in the imperial palace were used as wet nurses to suckle them and eunuchs employed to watch over them, but they still manage to have their every whim catered for and are extremely forceful characters whose affection has to be earned by its owner. Once given one could not wish for a more devoted companion.

Below The Tibetan Spaniel is probably descended from the Lhaso Apso and Chinese spaniels. It was considered to be sacred and led a carefully guarded life in palaces and monasteries.

Varieties: from left to right, sable, biscuit and white, black and tan, brown and white, red, white, brown and black.

This is not a kennel dog, but a companion which appreciates the freedom of the house.

The ideal weight for the Pekingese should not exceed 5kg (11lb), bitches 5.5kg (12lb). There are also what are known as "sleeve" Pekes (so named, it is believed, because they were concealed in the large sleeves of the mandarins' gowns), which weigh no more than 2.75kg (6lb). The breed comes in various acceptable colours and markings, except for the outlawed albino or liver. Parti-colours should be evenly broken.

Left *The Japanese Chin probably descends mainly from the Pekinese and the Tibetan Spaniel. It first arrived in Europe during the 15th century.*

115

THE CAVALIER KING CHARLES SPANIEL

A LARGER TOY BREED, the Cavalier is immensely popular because of its good temperament and attractive appearance. It is a faithful, loving companion, reliable with children, and draws enormous entries in dog show classes.

Alas, there must be many who set out to get either a Cavalier or a King Charles Spaniel and come home with the other simply because they do not know the difference. In fact, the Cavalier is larger and, unlike the King Charles's well-domed skull, the Cavalier's is almost flat between the ears, and its stop is much shallower. It is a matter of choice, for they both share the same characteristics.

The Cavalier and the King Charles both trace back to common stock. The King Charles can trace its ancestry to Japan 2000 years ago and became popular at the Stuart court in 16th-century England. It has often been related how King Charles II of England spent more time playing with his spaniels in council chambers than attending to affairs of state and how he would take his pets into the bedchamber.

In fact, the King Charles was more like the Cavalier, having a longer nose. It was when shorter nosed dogs became fashionable that the King Charles as we know it came about, the old type almost disappearing, until in the late 1920s a group of devotees determined to bring back the older type – which they wisely prefixed with the word "Cavalier".

The Cavalier weighs 5.4–8kg (12–18lb) and comes in a number of attractive colours: black and tan, ruby (whole-coloured rich red), Blenheim (rich chestnut markings well broken up on a pearly white ground) and tricolour (black-and-white well spaced, broken up).

Varieties: *from left to right, Blenheim, ruby, tricolour and black and tan.*

Cavalier King Charles

KEY FACTS

Character Sporting, affectionate and fearless. Ideal pet, good with children.
Exercise Should not be kennelled out of doors, but the Cavalier enjoys a good walk with its owner.
Grooming Daily brushing with bristle brush. Eyes should be kept clear of tear streaks.
Feeding Approximately ¾ can (400g size) of a branded meaty product, with biscuit added in equal part by volume.
Longevity Good.
Faults Include possible over-popularity resulting in some poor stock – so choose your breeder with care.

Above The Cavalier King Charles has a flattish head between the ears, and comes in a variety of colours, including Blenheim (chestnut and white), shown here.

Left The King Charles Spaniel has a high-domed head and very long ears.

THE CHIHUAHUA: LONG-COAT AND SMOOTH-COAT

Left The long-coated Chihuahua. Despite their small size, Chihuahuas are very intelligent and brave.

KEY FACTS

Character Devoted, clannish, keenly intelligent. Splendid miniature guard.
Exercise Don't be misled into thinking that Chihuahuas are just for carrying. They can be, but you would be surprised how much they enjoy a good walk.
Grooming Brush with a soft brush and rub down with a velvet pad or chamois leather to make the coat gleam. Don't neglect tear stains around eyes.
Feeding ⅓–½ can (400g size) of a branded meaty product (400g size), with biscuit added in equal part by volume.
Longevity Can live well into the 'teens, but the particularly tiny specimens rarely do so.
Faults Include tipped or broken-down ears.

THE CHIHUAHUA is the smallest dog in the world, its ideal weight being 0.9–2.7kg (2–6lb), but there are many specimens below or above the standard weight which make good pets. Whatever their weight, Chihuahuas do not con-sider themselves small dogs. They think they are enormous, and are foolhardy enough to take on all comers. It is typical of a Chihuahua to race up and growl, for instance, at a Doberman which, if it is lucky, will treat it with disdain.

Although it will get on with other pets, the Chihuahua much prefers to be with its own kind. It adores its owner, although the pup or newcomer will take a little time to give its wholehearted trust, and is determined from the outset to become the VIP member of the household. It may be small, but it is supremely intelligent.

The Chihuahua is called after the Mexican state of that name, and is reputed to have been the sacred dog of the Incas. From the evidence it is probable that the hairless dogs which came to South America from China had a part in producing the delightful Chihuahua.

SMOOTH- AND LONG-COATS

Chihuahuas come with both smooth- and long-coats, and which you choose is a matter of sheer preference. Some people like smooth-coated dogs, others like the glamour of a long-coat, or simply enjoy having a luxuriant coat to brush. At one time the two types were allowed to interbreed, so that one might have both smooth- and long-coats in the same litter, but this is no longer permissible and there are separate show classes for the two varieties. The long-coats are currently more popular.

The Chihuahua comes in any colour or mixture of colours, including blue and chocolate. Eyes are dark or, in the case of the chocolate, ruby. Light eyes in light colours are allowed.

Right The Papillon, so-called for its wing-shaped ears. Its origins are unclear, but it may be descended in part from the Chihuahua. It was a very fashionable breed in Europe.

Varieties: top from left to right, cream, fawn, black and white: bottom from left to right, brown and tan, brown and white and black and tan.

Chihuahua: Long Coat

THE ITALIAN GREYHOUND

THE GRACEFUL Italian Greyhound is a greyhound in miniature, but more slender in all proportions. It is a very loving, sensitive house-pet which nonetheless enjoys plenty of exercise. However, it is frightening that it was recently publicized as the "ideal pet": remember that it is a pet for extra-careful people who understand that clumsiness could lead to broken legs, that the little Italian feels the cold and always needs a coat in chill weather, and that harsh words cause this dainty pet very much pain.

KEY FACTS

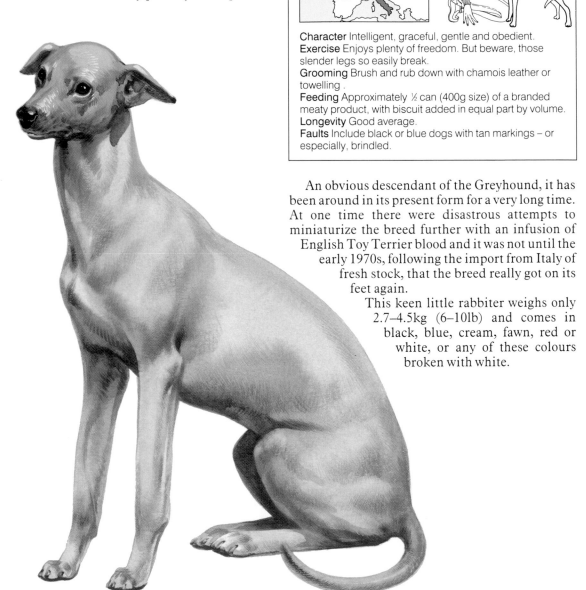

Character Intelligent, graceful, gentle and obedient.
Exercise Enjoys plenty of freedom. But beware, those slender legs so easily break.
Grooming Brush and rub down with chamois leather or towelling .
Feeding Approximately ½ can (400g size) of a branded meaty product, with biscuit added in equal part by volume.
Longevity Good average.
Faults Include black or blue dogs with tan markings – or especially, brindled.

An obvious descendant of the Greyhound, it has been around in its present form for a very long time. At one time there were disastrous attempts to miniaturize the breed further with an infusion of English Toy Terrier blood and it was not until the early 1970s, following the import from Italy of fresh stock, that the breed really got on its feet again.

This keen little rabbiter weighs only 2.7–4.5kg (6–10lb) and comes in black, blue, cream, fawn, red or white, or any of these colours broken with white.

Varieties: from left to right, fawn, black and white, white, cream, black, red and blue.

Right The Whippet is descended from the Greyhound crossed with terrier blood. It was first bred in the 19th century in the north of England, for hare coursing.

121

THE AIREDALE TERRIER

Left Although a typical terrier, the Welsh terrier adapts well to family life.

Below The Lakeland Terrier is related to the Welsh Terrier, which shares common ancestors with the Airedale.

KEY FACTS

Character Friendly, courageous and intelligent. Good with children.
Exercise Needs plenty, particularly if kept in town.
Grooming Daily brushing with a stiff brush. Professional stripping twice a year.
Feeding Approximately 1–1½ cans (400g size) of a branded meaty product, with biscuit added in equal part by volume.
Longevity Good average.
Faults Include pendulous ears, or ears set too high.

THE AIREDALE is the largest of the terriers and what could be described as a "True Brit", named after its place of origin in the Aire valley (dale) of Yorkshire. Yorkshire gamekeepers kept terriers to control vermin and these were undoubtedly crossed with the Otterhound to produce the Airedale. It is an excellent ratter, ducker and can even be trained to the gun and, of course, for obedience.

The Airedale has a steady temperament, likes to be part of the family and makes a splendid playmate for children. However, while some Airedales are docile as lambs there are those which are not averse to a good scrap with other dogs, chasing motor-bikes and making something of a nuisance of themselves. So it is vitally important to buy a pup from a kennel which breeds for both quality and temperament. A good Airedale is a joy and a pleasure to behold. However, the show Airedale does have to be hand-stripped, an art which must be learnt by the owner if a certain amount of expense is not to be incurred.

Incidentally, the Airedale worked as a police dog before the German Shepherd largely took over that role. It has also been a patrol dog for the dock and railway police and served in the armed forces.

Despite its size, 58–61cm (23–24in), bitches 56–59cm (22–23in), the Airedale is a dog that can live happily in town, provided that it receives sufficient exercise.

Colours are body-saddle black or grizzle at the top of the neck and top surface of tail. All other parts tan.

Varieties: from top to bottom, black and tan and grizzle.

THE NORFOLK TERRIER (AND NORWICH TERRIER

Above The Border Terrier came from the England/Scotland border. It is a good hunter, hardy and fast, and has been used to improve other breeds.

Varieties: from top to bottom, wheaten, red, grizzle and black and tan.

KEY FACTS

Character Lovable, hardy and active. Good family pet.
Exercise Like most terriers, these little dogs like nothing better than a good scamper in the country, but will adapt to town life.
Grooming Routine brushing and combing. Some trimming.
Feeding ½–1 can (400g size) of a branded meaty product, with biscuit added in equal part by volume.
Longevity Good lifespan.
Faults Include tendency to chase small livestock, if unchecked. (They love farm life and can be taught to guard rather than chase stock.)

THE NORFOLK AND NORWICH TERRIERS are practically identical except for their ears: the Norfolk's are lop, the Norwich's prick. The Norfolk also has a slightly longer neck. A useful trick for identifying the breeds is to remind oneself that the Norfolk's ears are flat like the county, and that the upright-eared Norwich is like the towers of Norwich Cathedral!

The Norwiches and Norfolks were developed in England in the 1880s. Earlier, in the 1860s, a Colonel Vaughan of Ballybrick in Ireland had hunted with a pack of small red terriers evolved from the Irish terrier from which the many resulting out-crossed prick-eared and drop-eared terriers came about. At one time the ears of the drop-eared terriers were cropped, but following an outcry the practice became illegal.

Also credited with the evolution of the Norwich is Jodrell Hopkins, a horse dealer from Trumpington, Cambridge. Mr Hopkins owned a bitch, some of the pups of which were acquired by his employee, Frank Jones. Jones crossed them with other terriers, including the Glen of Imaal Terrier, and called the progeny "Jones" or "Trumpington" terriers. These dogs were particularly popular with the undergraduates at Cambridge University who called them "Jones ter-

Norfolk Terrier

riers" and it was not until after World War I that the name Norwich terrier came into use.

In 1964 the Norwich and the Norfolk terriers were recognized as one breed by the United Kingdom Kennel Club and in January 1979 the two dogs were awarded separate status. Hardy and good with children, the Norfolks make ideal pets.

The Norfolk and the Norwich stand 25–26cm (10in) and come in all shades of red, wheaten, black-and-tan or grizzle. White marks or patches are out.

Right *The Norwich Terrier, which differs from the Norfolk only in its prick ears.*

THE BULL TERRIER

AS WITH MOST BULL BREEDS, people seem either to love them or hate them. There are those who consider the Bull Terrier the ugliest creature imaginable, others who find them tremendously appealing. They were bred for fighting and the instinct is still strong enough for them to take on all comers – and win. Therefore, they are not really a dog for the beginner. However, let it be said that they make devoted and loyal pets, are sound with children (particularly the bitch), and that, provided they are firmly but kindly disciplined, and kept in the right

environment – *not* an apartment – the owner should have no problems.

When bull baiting was outlawed by Parliament in 1835, a band of fanciers (including James Hinks of Birmingham, England) were determined to maintain the breed and improve it, while retaining its great strength and tenacity. This was achieved by crossing the White English Terrier with the Bulldog and the Dalmatian, thereby producing a new breed of English Bull Terriers. It was only later that the Brindle Bull Terrier came on the scene.

The Bull Terrier has no official height or weight limit, but its standard calls for maximum substance for size of dog consistent with quality and sex.

Colours are white, black, brindle, red, fawn and tri-colour.

Left *There is no official size range for the Bull Terrier. The example illustrated is a Miniature.*

Below *The Bull Terrier comes in a number of colours, including white.*

KEY FACTS

Character Described as the gladiator of the canine race. Super pet for the devotee, but not for beginners.
Exercise Active dog that needs a great deal of exercise.
Grooming Brushing and rub down will keep the coat in good condition.
Feeding Approximately 1½ cans (400g size) of a branded meaty product, with biscuit added in equal part by volume.
Longevity Average.
Faults Include obstinacy, and blue or partly blue eyes.

Varieties: top from left to right, white and black: middle from left to right, red and fawn: bottom from left to right, brindle and tricolour.

THE STAFFORDSHIRE BULL TERRIER

Left The Bulldog was one of the partners mated to breed the Staffordshire Bull Terrier during the 19th century. Its contribution of short legs, deep chest, and an amiable disposition toward humans have helped the "Staffy" gain a devoted following.

THE POPULAR "STAFFY" has, like the Bull Terrier, its band of devotees and it certainly makes a devoted household pet that can be trusted with children. It cannot, however, always be trusted with other dogs and you may sometimes find it an embarrassment to be on the end of the lead of a pet which is straining to "have a go" at its fellows. A good idea is to take it to a dog training class when it is a pup so that it becomes accustomed to other dogs.

The Staffordshire Bull Terrier is the product of a Bulldog and terrier mating in the 19th century. It is thought that the Bulldog's partner might well have been the Old English Black-and-tan Terrier which preceded the Manchester Terrier, a breed which has been recognized by the United Kingdom Kennel Club since the 1930s.

AMERICAN STAFFORDSHIRE TERRIER

The "Staffy" is not the same as the infamous Pit Bull Terrier, the correct name for which is the American Staffordshire Terrier. (At one time the

KEY FACTS

Character Courageous, intelligent, affectionate. Super pet, wonderful with children, but has a liking for fights.
Exercise Boundless energy. Like the Bull Terrier, best in a controlled country situation.
Grooming A brush and rub down will keep the coat gleaming.
Feeding 1–1½ cans (400g size) of a branded meaty product, with biscuit added in equal part by volume.
Longevity Good average.
Faults Include full, drop or pricked ears.

American Kennel Club did allow the American "Staffy" to be shown with the Staffordshire Bull Terrier and crossbreeding of the two was permitted.) The Pit Bull was evolved in England from the mating of an English Bulldog and an English terrier, the result being a much heavier dog altogether than the Staffordshire Bull. Once it had reached the United States in 1870 it soon became known as the Pit Dog, Pit Bull Terrier and Yankee Terrier. I have heard of Pit Bulls that are as gentle as lambs, but the majority are not and they are not recommended as pets.

The Staffordshire Bull Terrier weighs 13–17kg (28–38lb), bitches 11–15.5kg (24–34lb), and stands 11–15.5cm (14–16in) high, these heights being related to the weights. Colours are red, fawn, white, black or blue, or any one of these colours with white; and any shade of brindle or of brindle with white. Don't buy a "Staffy" that is black-and-tan or liver colour if you intend to exhibit in the show ring, for those colours are considered undesirable.

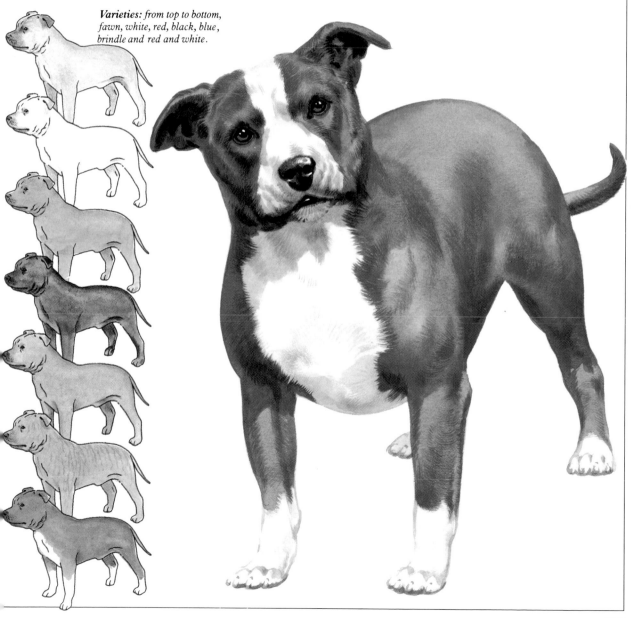

Varieties: from top to bottom, fawn, white, red, black, blue, brindle and red and white.

THE WEST HIGHLAND WHITE TERRIER

THE POPULAR "Westie" is a true Scot sharing common ancestry with the Dandie Dinmont and Cairn Terrier. In the early 1900s many such terriers, which were bred to hunt vermin and other small animals were banded together, but we do know that in the late 19th century a Colonel Malcolm of Poltalloch, had a strain of white Scottish terriers, known as the Poltalloch or Roseneath terrier.

An adaptable, happy pet that will live indoors or in an outside kennel – but infinitely prefers to share the fireside – the "Westie" has become immensely popular and there are many poor specimens about, so it is well worth seeking out a good breeder if you are thinking of acquiring one.

Standing approximately 28cm (11in) high at the withers, and weighing 7–8.5kg (15–18lb) the West Highland White Terrier comes in one colour only, white, so don't, as so many people do, mix him up with the black Scottish Terrier (the "Scottie"), once known as the Aberdeen Terrier. The West Highland is also shorter in the back, and has a shorter head and smaller ears, than the Scottie. Its eyes should be dark and widely set and its ears small and pointed.

Top right The Cairn Terrier *shares a common ancestry with the West Highland. It was not until the 20th century that these small terrier breeds were distinguished from one another.*

Right The Dandie Dinmont, *originating from the England/Scotland border, is also related to the Cairn.*

KEY FACTS

Character Game, hardy, adaptable and attractive pet that gets on with children and other pets.

Exercise A born ratter and hunter, this keen terrier will adapt to suburban living, but do ensure that it gets the exercise it deserves.

Grooming Daily brushing and combing. However, like the Airedale, this fellow needs twice-yearly hand stripping and constant work on its coat it you aspire to the show ring.

Feeding Approximately 1 can (400g size) of a branded meaty product, with biscuit added in equal part by volume.

Longevity Good.

Faults Include a nose that projects forward, light coloured eyes.

SETTERS

Below The Gordon Setter is black with tan markings. Its ancestry probably includes Bloodhound and Collie blood.

SETTERS ARE SUPERB gundogs and make ideal pets. They are not by any manner of means guard dogs, and would be more likely to persuade a burglar to come and play than repel his entry!

Confusion sometimes exists as to which setter is which. In fact, the Irish (or Red) Setter is the most popular and, if one is frank, the most scatty, especially in youth. It is ideal as a family pet, as a gundog, or in stables, where it can run with the horses. It evolved from crossing Irish Water Spaniels, Springer Spaniels, English and Gordon Setters and the Spanish Pointer.

The Irish Setter began life as a red-and-white dog and, indeed, Irish Red and White Setters are now making their mark as a separate breed.

The English Setter, again good with children and a first-class gundog, has distinctive black-and-white, lemon-and-white, liver-and-white or tricolour markings, and is reckoned to have evolved from spaniels, while the Gordon Setter, which is coal-black with tan markings (described as the colour of a ripe horse-chestnut) is the only native Scottish gundog, bred at Gordon Castle, Banffshire, the seat of the Dukes of Richmond and Gordon and originally known as the Gordon Castle Setter. The Collie and Bloodhound are attributed in its make-up.

Varieties: left from top to bottom, black and white, liver and white, lemon and white and tricolour: right from top to bottom, Irish (red), red and white, Gordon.

KEY FACTS

Character Beautiful, untiring, ready to hunt. Good with children, horses and other animals.
Exercise An exuberant animal which it would be cruel to keep in a confined environment.
Grooming Daily grooming with a stiff brush. You will also need a steel comb to avoid tangles. Ask the breeder about trimming.
Feeding At least 1½ cans (400g size) of a branded meaty product, with biscuit added in equal part by volume.
Longevity Can live into the 'teens.
Faults Include over-exuberance (should you consider that a fault).

Not so frequently seen as the Irish and English variety, the Gordon has possibly the steadier temperament of the three, being easy-going, calm and docile. It is also a methodical hunter.

Setters stand about 65–68cm (25½–27in) high, bitches 61–65cm (24–25½in) and, in common with the Labrador and Golden Retriever, are an ideal choice for the family wishing to combine a good gundog with a first-class family pet. However, they need plenty of freedom, and do not take to being confined in a small area.

Right The English Setter is probably descended from the spaniels. Black and white markings are one of a variety of colours acceptable in this breed.

Irish Red Setter

133

THE WEIMARANER

KEY FACTS

Character Good temperament and stamina. Excels at obedience and agility.
Exercise An exuberant dog that needs plenty of exercise and an outlet for keen intelligence.
Grooming Daily brushing.
Feeding 1½–2½ cans (400g size) of a branded meaty product, with biscuit added in equal part by volume.
Longevity Good average.
Faults Include the possibility that the dog could be more intelligent than its owner, with resultant problems.

NICKNAMED THE SILVER GHOST, the Weimaraner has been both police dog and guard dog. It was, in fact, purpose bred as a gundog at the Weimar court in Germany in the late 18th century, the defunct St Hubert Hounds, Bloodhounds and Pointers having a hand in its make-up. Since the early 1950s it has gained tremendous popularity in both Britain and America, where breed members have shone in the show ring both in beauty and obedience classes. The Weimaraner has also been widely sought after as a family pet, but here problems can arise for, although it is an affectionate animal, it is really not a beginner's dog and without proper training will assume control. It can live in town provided it receives sufficient exercise, but is certainly best when its keen intelligence has some satisfying task to keep it occupied.

Below The Hungarian Viszla is a breed with exceptional tracking and retrieving qualities, and it also makes a good family pet. Its ancestry dates back to the Middle Ages.

Varieties: from top to bottom, mouse grey, silver grey and roe grey.

The Weimaraner is a good-sized dog standing 61–69cm (24–27in) at the withers, bitches 56–64cm (22–25in), and is generally – and preferably – a distinctive silver grey in colour, though shades of mouse or roe grey are permissible, blending to a lighter shade on head and ears. Sometimes a dark eel stripe appears along the back.

Right *The Weimaraner has a good temperament, but is highly intelligent and needs expert training.*

THE WATER SPANIEL: IRISH AND AMERICAN

Varieties: from left to right, liver and chocolate.

The Irish Water Spaniel

AN ENCHANTING-LOOKING ANIMAL, the Irish Water Spaniel is a first-class water dog skilled at wild-fowling and trainable as an all-round gundog. It does however need obedience training from an early age and to be taught to get on with other animals. Nonetheless, it is affectionate and makes a good pet. It is also a better watch dog than most gundogs.

Like the Standard Poodle, which also began life as a water retriever, the Irish Water Spaniel evolved in Ireland from several spaniel breeds towards the latter part of the 19th century.

The American Water Spaniel, which is frankly more spaniel-like in appearance, but has the same

qualities as the Irish, is believed to have evolved from the crossing of the Irish Water with, as would appear likely, a smaller spaniel or with the Curly Coated Retriever. It is sometimes called the Boykin Spaniel after one of the pioneers of the breed.

The Irish Water Spaniel stands 53–58cm (21–23in), bitches 51–56cm (20–22in) and has one colour only: rich, dark liver with a purplish tint or bloom that is peculiar to the breed and is sometimes referred to as puce-liver.

The American Water Spaniel stands 38–46cm (15–18in) and may be solid liver in colour or dark chocolate, possibly with white on toes or chest.

KEY FACTS

Character Devotion, endurance, first-class water dog. Good pet, but can be tricky with strangers.
Exercise Needs plenty. Not an ideal choice for an enclosed environment.
Grooming Regular brushing. Neglect this and its coat will mat. Some stripping.
Feeding Approximately 1–1½ cans (400g size) of a branded meaty product, with biscuit added in equal part by volume.
Longevity Good.
Faults Include tendency to fight other dogs.

Above The Irish Water Spaniel is dark liver in colour. Its curly coat needs regular attention.

Left Although classed as a separate breed, the only obvious difference between the Curly-coated and Flat-coated retrievers is their coats. The Curly-coated is also a slightly heavier build.

THE GOLDEN RETRIEVER

THE BEAUTIFUL Golden Retriever is kindly and trust-worthy with children. It may be kennelled outdoors, but infinitely prefers to be inside as one of the family. Like the Labrador Retriever, it is a good all-purpose dog which ideally combines the role of owner's gundog with family pet. It works well in obedience and, being easy to train, is popular as a Guide Dog for the Blind.

It is generally accepted that the Golden Retriever evolved from a litter of retriever-cross-spaniel pups born on Lord Tweedmouth's Scottish estate in 1860. However, the rumour persists that their true ancestry sprang from a troupe of performing Russian shepherd dogs which his lordship saw performing in a circus at Brighton, Sussex.

The story goes that, so impressed was Lord Tweedmouth with the dogs, he purchased the entire troupe, subsequently adding Bloodhound blood to improve the "nose".

The Golden Retriever stands 56–61cm (22–24in) at the withers, bitches 51–56cm (20–22in), and comes in any shade of gold or cream. A few white hairs on the chest only are permissible.

Varieties: from left to right, light gold, cream and dark gold.

Left *The Chesapeake Bay Retriever is thought to be descended from Flat- and Curly-coated Retrievers and Newfoundlands. It has webbed feet and a thick, oily coat and is an excellent swimmer.*

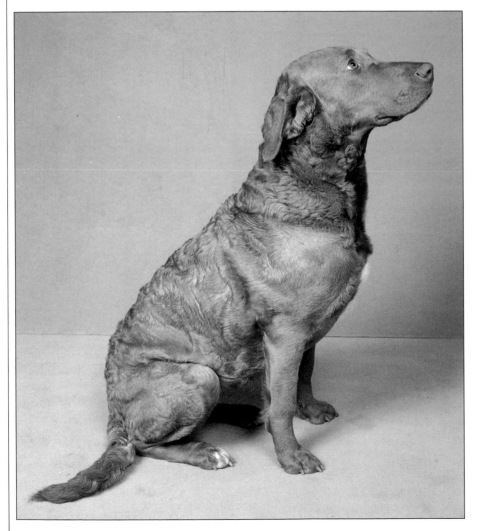

Above The Golden Retriever combines the qualities of gundog and family pet.

KEY FACTS

Character Kindly expression with temperament to match. Good all-purpose gundog and family pet.
Exercise Plenty of exercise to keep this dog fit, happy and in good shape.
Grooming Regular brushing.
Feeding At least 1½ cans (400g size) of a branded meaty product, with biscuit added in equal part by volume.
Longevity Good average.
Faults Cowhocks are highly undesirable.

THE LABRADOR RETRIEVER

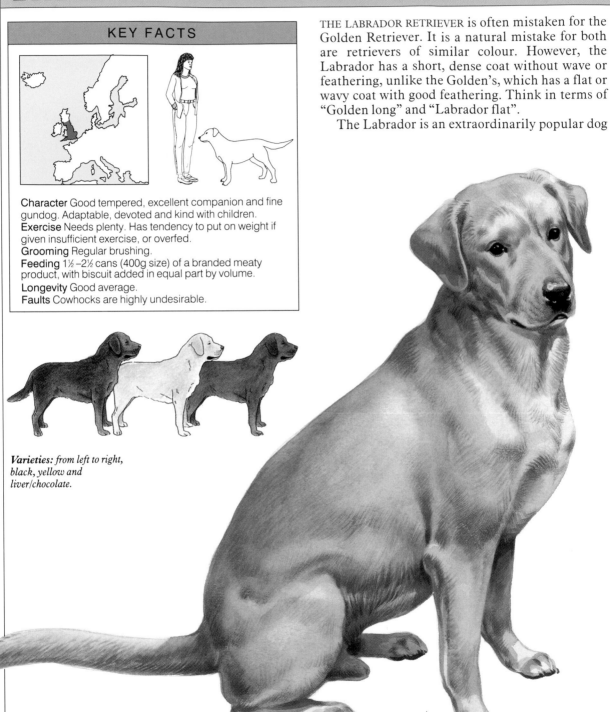
Varieties: from left to right, black, yellow and liver/chocolate.

THE LABRADOR RETRIEVER is often mistaken for the Golden Retriever. It is a natural mistake for both are retrievers of similar colour. However, the Labrador has a short, dense coat without wave or feathering, unlike the Golden's, which has a flat or wavy coat with good feathering. Think in terms of "Golden long" and "Labrador flat".

The Labrador is an extraordinarily popular dog

and justifiably so for it is an excellent gundog that makes a fine family pet. It is somewhat exuberant in adolescence, but soon settles down and is extremely adaptable. However, it is important that it receives sufficient exercise. There are an awful lot of overweight Labradors around – particularly spayed bitches which are overfed and taken out for exercise too seldom.

FISHERMAN'S FRIEND

The Labrador Retriever comes from Newfoundland where its original task was to help land the nets of fishermen, and its ability to swim survives. It has certainly existed in its present form since the 1830s, if not well before. Its present-day roles include police work, sniffing out drugs and explosives, and acting as Guide Dogs for the Blind.

The Labrador Retriever stands 56–57cm (22–22½in), bitches 54–56cm (21½in), and may be wholly black, yellow or liver/chocolate. Yellows range from light cream to red fox. Blacks and yellows are most popular, yellows being more plentiful nowadays than the blacks which some say are the better gundogs.

Above *The Flat-coated Retriever can be distinguished by its longer coat, which is often wavy, and the feathering on its legs and tail.*

Left *The Labrador Retriever has a flat, dense coat. It is most commonly either yellow or black, but chocolate brown occurs as well.*

THE COCKER SPANIEL

Left The American Cocker Spaniel, showing the slightly wavy coat and distinctive trousers characteristic of the breed.

Varieties: from left to right, golden, black, red, red and white, black and white and blue.

KEY FACTS

Character The "Merry Cocker" has an ever-wagging tail, is beautiful, intelligent, obedient and a first-class family pet.
Exercise Originally bred for hunting, the Cocker needs and enjoys plenty of exercise, particularly as, with its love of food, it can be in danger of losing its waistline.
Grooming Daily brushing and combing to avoid tangles. Mind those ears don't drop into the food bowl and become matted. Many owners peg them back at feed time.
Feeding 1–1½ cans (400g size) of a branded meaty product, with biscuit added in equal part by volume.
Longevity Can live into the 'teens.
Faults Include prominent cheek bones.

VILLAR, AN AUTHORITY on the Cocker Spaniel, once wrote this sensible appraisal: "There is no more pleasant dog, nor one more affectionate and lively than the Cocker. His well developed psychology makes him extremely interesting. The qualities of intelligence, goodness and cunning are all tied up together within him. He obeys not through servility but by sharing ideas with his master, whose slightest intention he is able to guess. He is most faithful, and also an excellent guard dog, wary of any suspicious sound and, if necessary, confronts an intruder with courage."

The Cocker, known in America as the English Cocker, in fact originated in Spain and can trace its ancestry back at least to the 14th century. It has been used in falconry and, while its task is generally to flush out game, it will also retrieve. It is a gentle, family dog and debatably one of the most beautiful in puppyhood. It responds to firm but kind training from an early age, and is an enthusiastic worker. There were some temperament problems with the goldens a few years ago, but hopefully these have now been eradicated.

Above The English Springer
Spaniel is one of the largest of
the spaniels. Its name comes
from the fact that it used to be
used to flush out or 'spring'
game.

The Cocker stands 39–41cm (15½–16in), bitches 38–39cm (15–15½in). Weight approximately 12.7–14.5kg (28–32lb). Colours are various, but in self-colours no white is allowed except on the chest.

The American Cocker is smaller than the English Cocker and has a silky, flat or slightly wavy coat and distinctive trousers. Bred in England, but developed in the United States where it is immensely popular, the American Cocker is also an excellent gundog and family pet and is debatably a more showy animal than the Cocker Spaniel. The American Cocker stands at 36–39cm (14–15in), bitches at 34–36cm (13–14in), and weighs about 12kg (26½lb). It occurs in a variety of colours. It is smaller than other hunting dogs, and is now usually kept as a pet.

THE FOXHOUND

Varieties: from top to bottom, black, fawn and white, fawn and white, tan and white and red, black and white.

Left *The typical black, tan and white colouring of the English Foxhound.*

ATTRACTIVE THOUGH IT MAY BE, the Foxhound is entirely unsuitable as a household pet. Indeed Foxhounds are not exhibited in the show ring in England except in a special hound show. It is however a contender in the show ring in America.

Foxhounds are invariably the property of a fox-hunting pack and are described in couples, for example, "fifty couples of hounds", and the nearest they ever get to a domestic environment is in puppyhood, when they may be "puppy walked" by a member of the public.

The Foxhound is a descendant of the former and heavier St Hubert Hound, which was brought to England by the Norman William the Conqueror and from another extinct hound, the Talbot. St Hubert, or Hubertus, Hounds took their name from the patron saint of hunters, associated in legend with an 8th-century bishop of Liège in Belgium.

The American Foxhound evolved from a pack of foxhounds taken to America by Robert Brooke in

KEY FACTS

Character Attractive, noisy hunter, which does not fit into a domestic environment.
Exercise It is a hunter – enough said.
Grooming Groom with a hound glove.
Feeding Foxhounds are not reared on domestic pet food but trencher-fed with horse flesh and mash comprising oatmeal and known as "pudding".
Longevity Good average.
Faults Include tail turned forward over back.

1650. George Washington is also credited with importing foxhounds from Britain and some fine specimens from France in 1785. We see the result of the cross-breeding of these English and French hounds in the American Foxhound of today.

Hounds stand 58.5cm (23in), bitches slightly less. No colour is described as bad for a Foxhound.

THE BEAGLE

Varieties: from left to right, tan and white, tan, grey and white, brown and white and fawn and white.

KEY FACTS

Character Happy, lovable, "naughty" little dog that probably shouldn't be kept as a pet, but often is.
Exercise Revels in it.
Grooming The Beagle's weatherproof coat requires little or no grooming.
Feeding 1–1½ cans (400g size) of a branded meaty product, with biscuit added in equal part by volume.
Longevity Can live into the 'teens.
Faults Include destructiveness, disobedience and slinking off.

THE BEAGLE is an attractive small dog, with a penchant for wandering off, true to its hound instincts. It is not the most obedient of dogs. Indeed it can be noisy and a trifle tiresome, but it is nonetheless lovable and while many people will say that the right place for a Beagle is in a Beagle pack, I can think of more than one which has been a devoted household pet for 14 years or more. They are good with children, and usually very healthy – great fun to go for a walk with!

Beagles are an ancient breed, written about at least since the end of the 15th century. They have hunted hare for centuries, but have been used against various quarry in different countries of the world: wild pig in Ceylon, deer in Scandinavia, and jackal in the Sudan. They will retrieve, and in the USA they hunt by scent in Field Trials.

Standing a minimum of 33cm (13in), and no more than 40cm (16in), at the withers, the smart little Beagle can be any recognized hound colour except white, but the top of its stern must be white.

IRISH WOLFHOUND

Varieties: top from left to right, wheaten, steel grey, black and fawn: bottom from left to right, grey, white, red and brindle.

DESPITE THE WARNING that the Irish Wolfhound can be fierce, the dog is generally a gentle giant, the one many people declare as their favourite and would love to own were it not for its size and feeding cost.

The national dog of Ireland, of which the Irish are naturally proud, this wolfhound was originally bred as a wolf hunter and is believed to have arrived from the continent with invading Celts in the 3rd century BC.

Few can relate without a tear the story of Gelert the Irish Wolfhound, presented as a gift to Llewellyn ap Iorwerth, Prince of Wales, by King John in the early 1200s. One day Llewellyn went out hunting leaving Gelert to look after his son. On his return he noticed that the dog's mouth was covered with blood and saw no sign of his son. On impulse, believing that the dog had killed his son, he slew the dog with his sword – whereupon he heard a cry and found nearby not only his unharmed son, but the body of a wolf. Llewellyn had a statue erected in memory of Gelert the Irish Wolfhound.

The Irish Wolfhound has a minimum height of 79cm (31in), bitches 71cm (28in), its recognized colours being grey, brindle, red, black, pure white, fawn, wheaten and steel grey.

THE BLOODHOUND

DESPITE ITS ASSOCIATION with detective stories and formidable trekking, the Bloodhound is a supremely gentle and affectionate animal which adores children. It makes an excellent pet provided you have room to accommodate it and neighbours who won't be averse to the sound of baying, which can be a trifle disconcerting.

Although a good watchdog, the Bloodhound is not a guard, and its instinct is to follow scent and find its quarry – not to attack. It does of course need a large amount of exercise and owners are recommended to join a Bloodhound Club which organizes events. Apart from trekking, Bloodhounds attract good entries in the show ring.

One of the oldest, purest breeds of hound, the Bloodhound is believed to have originated from the Mediterranean area, possibly Greece or Italy, before the Christian era. It was brought to England by William the Conqueror in 1066 and there the modern type was developed.

The Bloodhound stands 66cm (26in), bitches 61cm (24in), and may be black-and-tan, liver-and-tan (red and tan) and red, sometimes flecked with white. A small amount of white is permissible on chest, feet and tip of tail.

Above The Bloodhound has formidable tracking ability, and needs a lot of exercise.

KEY FACTS

Character Superlative tracker, good with children and makes a good pet if you have room to accommodate it.
Exercise A great deal.
Grooming Use a hound glove daily.
Feeding About 2–2½ cans (400g size) of a branded meaty product, with biscuit added in equal part by volume.
Longevity Average.
Faults Prone to torsion – a build up of stomach gases. Be aware ot this, and contact a veterinarian immediately if hound is in trouble.

Above *The Otterhound is probably descended from the Bloodhound crossed with* terriers and the Griffons. Like the Bloodhound, it has an excellent nose, and is also good with children.

Varieties: *from top to bottom, black and tan, liver and red.*

THE BASENJI

THE BASENJI is a delightful choice of pet. It is odourless and clean, does not bark, giving only a kind of yodel, and is loyal, gentle and affectionate. It is good with children.

The Basenji has many appealing features. It washes itself like a cat, for example, and has a forehead full of what look like "concerned" wrinkles.

An ancient breed, dogs of Basenji type are

KEY FACTS

Character Gentle, odourless, good with horses, friendly with children.
Exercise Although a dog that essentially should be kept indoors with its owner – and not in an outside kennel – the Basenji was bred as a hunter, and enjoys the open spaces
Grooming Use a hound glove.
Feeding About 1½ cans (400g size) of a branded meaty product, with biscuit added in equal part by volume.
Longevity Average.
Faults Include dislike of rain, and the phenomenon of coming into season only once a year.

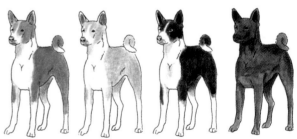

Varieties: from left to right, red and white, tan and white, black and white and black.

depicted in carvings on tombs of the pharaohs, and it is thought that such dogs were presented as tribute by travellers from the upper reaches of the Nile.

The breed had almost disappeared from view until the mid-19th century when it was discovered by explorers in the southern Sudan and the Congo. Most of today's stock has been imported from the Sudan, and also from Liberia in west Africa. Rumour has it that the Basenji is also to be found in the Malayan jungle and north of Katmandu.

The Basenji's ideal height is 43cm (17in) at withers, bitches 40cm (16in), and it comes in pure black-and-white, red-and-white, black, tan-and-white and tan-and-white with tan melon pips and mask. The white should be on feet, chest and tail tips. White legs, blaze and a white collar are optional.

THE AFGHAN HOUND

KEY FACTS

Character Beautiful, loyal, generally good with children, but can have its off moments, so best not to tease.
Exercise Need plenty of free running. Afghan racing is becoming a popular sport.
Grooming A Mason Pearson type brush of real bristle is ideal. Daily grooming must not be neglected.
Feeding 1½–2½ cans (400g size) of a branded meaty product, with biscuit added in equal part by volume.
Longevity Good average.
Faults Include possible bad temper in adolescence.

THE AFGHAN HOUND enjoys immense popularity and attracts large entries in show classes. A loyal and affectionate animal, it needs gentle but firm handling if it is not to attempt dominance; at the same time it must be understood that this is a dog that does not respond to bullying. In other words, let the dog know you love it, but stay the boss.

The Afghan is an ancient breed and the story is often told that it was one of the animals chosen to be taken into Noah's Ark.

A papyrus discovered in Sinai dated around 3000 BC was once thought to describe an early Afghan. In any event, this Greyhound-type dog found its way to Afghanistan where its long, shaggy coat developed to protect it against the climatic conditions.

The Afghan Hound stands at 68–74cm (27–29in), bitches 63–69cm (25–27in), and may be any colour.

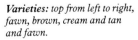

Varieties: top from left to right, fawn, brown, cream and tan and fawn.

THE DACHSHUND

THE DACHSHUND comes in two sizes, Standard and Miniature, and in no less than three coats, smooth-haired, long-haired and wire-haired. It also answers widely to the name of Teckel and as a Dackel, Dacksel and Badger Hound ("Dachs" means badger in German), the latter description being most appropriate for badger hunting was the purpose for which it was bred in its native Germany. What was wanted was a short legged hound with a keen sense of smell, courage and burrowing ability. The Dachshund is now famed for putting this latter ability to good use in its owner's garden!

The Dachshund makes an excellent pet, is supremely affectionate and generally likes children. However, it can be a little aggressive towards strangers and is a fine watchdog. It also has a very loud bark for its size – a real guard dog in miniature. Perhaps the only drawbacks to the breed are a tendency to disc trouble, if the dog is permitted to

Left *The Wire-haired Dachshund which was created by crossing the Smooth-hair with the Dandie Dinmont.*

Below *The Long-haired, which was created by crossing with the spaniel and a German breed called the Stoberhund.*

jump on and off chairs, and to be overweight.

Dachshunds have been around since at least the 16th century, having evolved from the oldest breeds of German hunting dogs, including the Bibarhund. The smooth-haired variety was the only one when the German Dachshund Club was formed in 1888. The wrinkled paws, then a characteristic of the breed, have been almost bred out. The wire-hair was designed by crossing with the Dandie Dinmont and other terriers, the long-hair by crossing the smooth-haired Dachshund with the spaniel and an obsolete German gundog called the Stoberhund.

All colours are allowed except in Dapples, which should be evenly marked all over – no white permissible, save for a rather undesirable small patch on the chest. Black-and-tan and red are the most popular colours.

Ideal weights are: Standards 9–12kg (20–26lb); Miniatures 4.5kg (10lb).

KEY FACTS

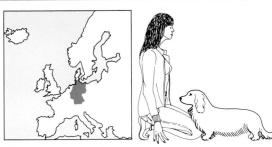

Character Intelligent, lively, courageous, obedient and affectionate.
Exercise Short, frequent walks help preserve the Dachshund's waistline.
Grooming Use a hound glove and rub down with a soft brush. A stiff-bristled brush and a comb need to be used on the long- and wire-haired varieties.
Feeding About ½ can (400g size) of a branded meaty product for the Miniature, ¾–1 can maximum for the Standard, with biscuit added in equal part by volume.
Longevity Some live into the 'teens.
Faults Too much hair on feet and hind dew claws.

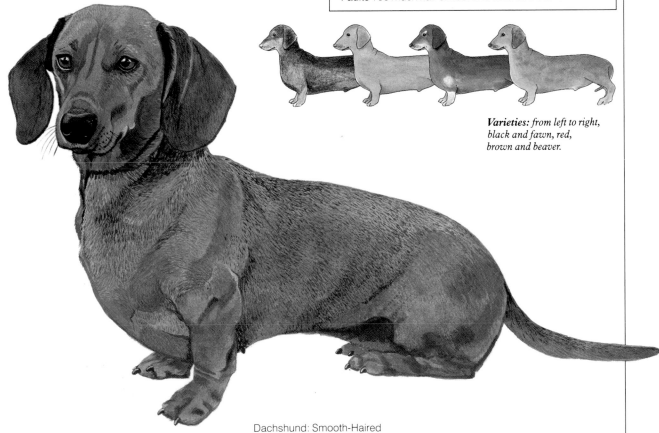

Varieties: from left to right, black and fawn, red, brown and beaver.

Dachshund: Smooth-Haired

THE GREYHOUND

THE GREYHOUND is a pure breed which does not appear to have changed a great deal since ancient Egyptian times, if we are to go by surviving carvings and paintings. It was among the first breeds to be trained to hunt. In more recent times it was highly prized among the nobility of Europe.

Although Greyhounds are bred as pets and for the show ring one tends to think of them predominantly as racers. Sadly, when that racing life is over, or should it end prematurely, this most docile of

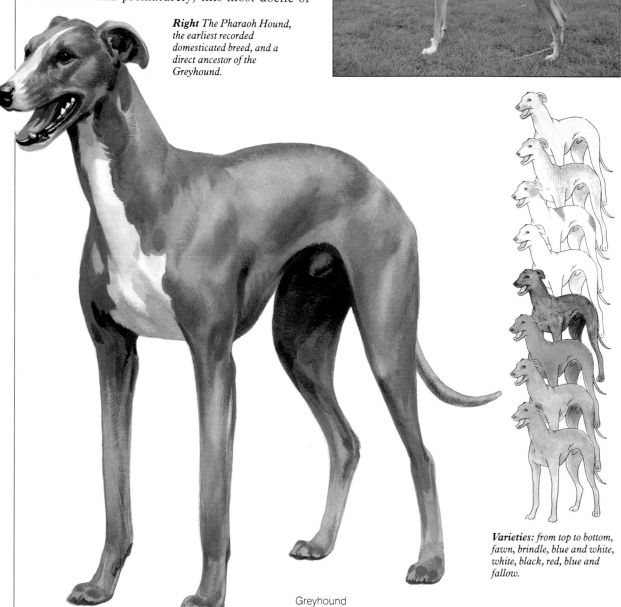

Right *The Pharaoh Hound, the earliest recorded domesticated breed, and a direct ancestor of the Greyhound.*

Varieties: *from top to bottom, fawn, brindle, blue and white, white, black, red, blue and fallow.*

Greyhound

Left The Saluki is another ancient hound. Like the Pharaoh Hound and Greyhound, it hunts by sight rather than scent. It is intelligent and gentle.

Below Greyhounds that have retired from racing make excellent household pets. Once out of training, they do not need a lot of exercise.

KEY FACTS

Character Has remarkable stamina and endurance, and is an adaptable, affectionate animal which makes a loyal and gentle pet.

Exercise Normal, regular walks are sufficient, but never let a Greyhound (especially an ex-racer) off the lead in a public place or anywhere where there is livestock. Ex-racers need de-training, or they will chase anything that moves.

Grooming Use hound glove every day.

Feeding 1½–2½ cans (400g size) of a branded meaty product, with biscuit added in equal part by volume. Greyhounds are used to sloppier foods than other breeds, and appreciate a thick slice of brown bread crumbled into milk at breakfast time and another drink of milk with a few biscuits at bedtime (most breeds enjoy bedtime biscuits as a treat).

Longevity Can live as pets to a fairly ripe age.

Faults Include a possible tendency to rheumatism and arthritis.

breeds often ends up in the veterinary laboratory or at least in need of a pet home. Bearing it in mind that after a period of de-training they do make excellent pets, and do not, despite their size, take up much space in the home, preferring to deposit themselves on a comfortable settee in a corner, they are well worth considering if you want a big dog.

Greyhounds come in black, white, red, blue, fawn, fallow, brindle, or any of these colours broken with white. There is no weight standard, but their ideal height is 71–76cm (28–30in), bitches 68–71cm (27–28in).

If you are interested in giving a home to a "retired" Greyhound and are not thinking in terms of the show ring, it would be sensible to enquire at your nearest Greyhound Racing Club.

INDEX

CREDITS

KEY T = TOP
B = BELOW
C = CENTRE
L = LEFT
B = BELOW

p.2: Marc Henrie. p.6: Marc Henrie. p.7: Marc Henrie. p.8: C.M. Dixon. p.9: Solitaire Photographic. p.10: T. Anne Marie Bazalik; B. Australian Overseas Information Service, London. p.12:C.M. Dixon. p.13: Marc Henrie. p.14: C.M. Dixon. p.15: E.T. Archive. p.16: Marc Henrie. p.17: Marc Henrie. p.18: Marc Henrie. p.19: T. Marc Henrie; B. Marc Henrie. p.21: Quarto Publishing plc. p.23: Marc Henrie. p.24: L. Ardea, London; R.Norvia Behling. p.25: Norvia Behling. p.26: L. Marc Henrie; R. Marc Henrie. p.27: L. Marc Henrie; R. Paul Forester. p.28–29: Solitaire Photographic. p.30: Marc Henrie. p.31: Wood Green Animal Shelters. p.32: Solitaire Photographic. p.33: Marc Henrie. p.37: Norvia Behling. p.39: Marc Henrie. p.40: T. Solitaire Photographic; B. Marc Henrie. p.41: Solitaire Photographic. p.44: L. Norvia Behling; R. Marc Henrie. p.45: J.S. Library International. p.46: Anne Marie Bazalik. p.47: C.M. Dixon: B. Kent & Donna Dannen. p.48: Norvia Behling. p.49: T. Kent & Donna Dannen; B. Marc Henrie. p.50: L. Marc Henrie; R. Kent & Donna Dannen. p.51: T. Marc Henrie; B. Solitaire Photographic. p.52: Marc Henrie. p.53: Solitaire Photographic. p.57: Anne Marie Bazalik. p.58: Solitaire Photographic. p.59: L. Marc Henrie; R. Marc Henrie. p.60: T. Marc Henrie; B. Marc Henrie. p.61: Marc Henrie. p.62: Agnes Leith. p.63: David C. Bitters. p.64: L. Marc Henrie; R. Ronald R. Domb. p.65: T. Marc Henrie; B. Marc Henrie. p.66: T. Marc Henrie; B. Solitaire Photographic. p.67: T. Solitaire Photographic; B. Brian A. Lewis. p.68: T. Solitaire Photographic; B. Solitaire Photographic. p.69: T. Marc Henrie; B. Marc Henrie. p.70: Solitaire Photographic (T & C). p.71. Marc Henrie (T & C). p.73: T. Solitaire Photographic; B. Anne Marie Bazalik. p.76: Marc Henrie. p.77: Solitaire Photographic. p.80: L. Marc Henrie; R. Solitaire Photographic. p.81: Marc Henrie. p.83: T. Marc Henrie; B. A.E. Linscott. p.85: L. Marc Henrie; R. Solitaire Photographic. p.86: T. Marc Henrie; B. Marc Henrie. p.89: T. Marc Henrie; B. Solitaire Photographic. p.90: Marc Henrie. p.91: Marc Henrie; p.92: T. Marc Henrie; B. Kent & Donna Dannen. p.93: Kent & Donna Dannen. p.95: T. Marc Henrie; B. Julie O'Neil – Photo/Nats. p.96: T. Marc Henrie; B. Anne Marie Bazalik. p.97: Marc Henrie. p.102: T. Julie O'Neil/Photo/Nats. B. Marc Henrie. p.104: T. David M. Stone – Photo/Nats; B. Marc Henrie. p.105: Solitaire Photographic. p.106: L. Solitaire Photographic; R. Marc Henrie. p.111: T. Solitaire Photographic; B. Solitaire Photographic. p.114: Marc Henrie. p.115: Solitaire Photographic. p.117: T. Marc Henrie; B. Marc Henrie. p.118: Marc Henrie. p.119: Marc Henrie. p.121: Anne Marie Bazalik. p.122: T. Marc Henrie; B. Marc Henrie. p.124: Marc Henrie. p.125: Marc Henrie. p.126: Marc Henrie. p.127: Solitaire Photographic. p.128: Marc Henrie. p.131: T. Marc Henrie; B. Marc Henrie. p.132: Marc Henrie. p.133: Solitaire Photographic. p.134: Marc Henrie. p.135: Marc Henrie. p.137: Solitaire Photographic. p.138: Solitaire Photographic. p.139: Anne Marie Bazalik. p.141: T. Solitaire Photographic; B. Marc Henrie. p.142: Marc Henrie. p.143: Marc Henrie. p.144–145 Solitaire and Marc Henrie p.148: T. Marc Henrie; B. Marc Henrie. p.152: T. Marc Henrie; B. Marc Henrie. p.154: Marc Henrie. p.155: L. Spectrum Colour Library; R. Marc Henrie.

Quarto extends its special thanks to Pet World, Bromley Road, London, for the loan of equipment used in some photographs.